CHRIST, CULTURE, AND THE PURSUIT OF PURITY

Authentic LOVE

AMY-JO GIRARDIER

truelovewaits.

LifeWay Press® Nashville, Tennessee

ISBN: 978-1-4300-6461-9
Item 005791915

Dewey Decimal Classification: 306.73
Subject Heading: CHRISTIAN LIFE \ SEXUAL ABSTINENCE \ GOSPEL

Printed in the United States of America

Student Ministry Publishing
LifeWay Resources
One LifeWay Plaza
Nashville, TN 37234-0144

We believe that the Bible has God for its author; salvation for its end; and truth, without any
mixture of error, for its matter and that all Scripture is totally true and trustworthy. To review
LifeWay's doctrinal guideline, please visit *www.lifeway.com/doctrinalguideline*.

Contents

About the Author

Amy-Jo Girardier is the Girls Minister at Brentwood Baptist Church in Brentwood, Tennessee. She has been serving in this role for 14 years and still can't believe this is what she gets to do for a job! Originally from Springfield, Illinois, Amy-Jo graduated from Southwest Baptist University and attended Southwestern Baptist Theological Seminary to pursue a Master's in Christian Education. She is the founding editor of *www.girlsminister.com*, a website created to connect and resource girls ministers, moms, and youth workers engaged in the girls ministry conversation. Amy-Jo has also written *Faithful One: A Study of 1 & 2 Thessalonians for Teen Girls* with LifeWay and serves on the LifeWay Girls Ministry Team.

In addition to ministry, Amy-Jo loves using technology, passing on her love of technology to others, drinking coffee, running, serving with her husband, Darrel, loving on her son, Scout, and chill-axing with her Boston Terrier, Diesel.

Special Thanks

Thank you to my husband, Darrel, and son, Scout, for the many sacrifices you made so I could participate in this incredible resource. Thanks to my first girls minister—my mom, Connie Jo Morgan, for praying and being a sounding board. And thanks to my pastor, Mike Glenn, who prays for me and cheers me on.

This study would not have been possible without the constant prayer support from what I affectionately call "TEAM AJ." There were people from around the world praying for me as I wrote, for my editorial team as they edited, and for my video team as they produced. Team AJ will continue to pray for you as you study this with your group. TEAM AJ: Mike Glenn, Scott and Paige Drennan, Carol Vicary, Lori Beth Horton, Jean Crosby, Karyn Caldwell, Julia Kasick, Bonita Wilson, Marty Girardier, Lorri Steiner, Aaron and Kelsey Kunz, Amy Bryant, Mark and Stacey Morgan, Rene Cook, Tiffany Evins, Robin Keels, Ellie Dowling, Ron and Debbie Bleankney, Rachel Williams, Holly Kunz, Katie Hathaway; Scott, Beth, and Elizabeth Harris; Chris, Christy, and Caroline White.

Thanks to the Brentwood Student Team for cheering me on: Garrett Gregory, Chris White, Karyn Caldwell, Julia Kasick, Evan Kunz, Chris Blanton, John Harland, Austin Woods, and Laura Galvez. Also, a special thanks to all the girls and leaders at Brentwood Baptist Church who were on my heart as I wrote this resource. My prayer is that it will be used for God's glory.

Thanks to Amy Byrd, Katie Wylie, and Amanda Craft on the LifeWay Girls Team for cheering me on! And of course, thanks to the editorial team and video team at LifeWay. Thanks to Ben Trueblood, John Paul Basham, Karen Daniel, Jennifer Siao, Sarah Nikolai, and the LifeWay Student team for their support, hard work, and for believing in me.

About This Study

Every day we are invited into a world where we can create, customize, and even change our identity. This is evidenced in the filters available to us on social media, and also in how we can change our appearances through the clothing, hair, and makeup industries. We become consumers in a culture that tells us we can have whatever we want whenever we want it.

Speaking directly to the hearts of girls, *Authentic Love: Christ, Culture, and the Pursuit of Purity* exposes culture's distorted messages about purity and love and reveals how God has created us for a lifestyle of personal holiness. Over the course of eight sessions, young women will examine attributes of holiness that shape our identity. They will be challenged to reject the self-serving influences of culture and embrace what it means to pursue holiness and reflect the character of Christ.

How to Use

PRESS PLAY

Begin each session watching the video from Amy-Jo as a group. Read the opening passage of Scripture and take a few minutes to discuss girls' answers to the questions that follow.

LET'S TALK

Start working through the following three sections: Culture, Identity in Christ, and Purity. The information in this portion of the study will guide girls to consider the cultural perspective to the topic of each session, and how we are to place our identity in Christ rather than let the culture define who we are and what we believe. Then, when we learn to root our identity in Christ, our lives will naturally reflect the personal holiness and purity Jesus calls us to.

The final section of Let's Talk is the Now What? section. Here, you can conclude your time as a group by leading girls through a few more discussion questions and then guiding them to practically apply Scripture to their lives.

ON YOUR OWN

The final page of each session is designed for girls to complete on their own sometime over the course of the following week as they reflect on what they learned in the group time.

LEADER GUIDE

The Leader Guide at the end of this book contains specific helps and tips for you, as leaders. Every group is different, so we want you to be able to adapt this study for your specific group of girls. With that in mind, this section includes a variety of ideas, helps, and tips for you as you walk through this study with girls, pointing them to Christ and encouraging them to glorify God by pursuing a life of holiness.

The Best Possible You

1 PETER 2:9-12

9 But you are a chosen race, a royal priesthood,
a holy nation, a people for His possession,
so that you may proclaim the praises
of the One who called you out of darkness
into His marvelous light.

10 Once you were not a people,
but now you are God's people;
you had not received mercy,
but now you have received mercy.

11 Dear friends, I urge you as strangers and temporary residents to abstain from fleshly desires that war against you. 12 Conduct yourselves honorably among the Gentiles, so that in a case where they speak against you as those who do what is evil, they will, by observing your good works, glorify God on the day of visitation.

WELCOME

Hey girls! I'm so excited to be spending the next eight weeks of this study with you! But first things first — let's get to know one another. I'll start us off. I'm Amy-Jo. I'm a girls minister from Nashville, Tennessee, and I love technology and drinking coffee. Before we move on, take a few minutes to introduce yourself to the girls in your group.

Press Play

Watch the Session 1 video. As Amy-Jo introduces the study, she shares how "The Best Possible You" is only possible in Christ.

DISCUSS

What did you think about the story of Amy-Jo's makeover from her friend Jenny on school picture day? Have you ever had a bad makeover? If so, share your story.

Do you ever get too engrossed in trying to post the perfect picture on Instagram? Explain.

How can we strive to perfect our hearts and minds as much as we try to create perfect photos?

In what ways can Christ give us a new heart and mind, making us a new creation?

Let's Talk

CULTURE

Our culture plays a significant role in our lives. We need to be aware of the messages it sends so that we can test them against the truth of God's Word. As we begin to discern what is true, we will find our identity in Christ rather than in the latest fad. We'll see that cultural trends are temporary and cannot sustain us.

Have you ever thought about what the best possible you would look like? Think about it: Every morning you get up and work on something to better yourself or get yourself closer to the best possible you.

Do you remember what your New Year's resolutions were? If so, list them here.

-loose weight
-closer to God
- School

Sometimes the resolutions we make have to do with our health or our attitude. Sometimes they have to do with a skill or involve checking a life experience off our list.

Nowadays, we have the added bonus of Pinterest, Snapchat, Instagram, and YouTube to help us figure out how to get the best eyebrow shape or the best room decor. You can spend hours finding new ways to use makeup tricks such as contouring, which is like a cheat code for enhancing your facial structure.

How often do you compare yourself to others? Your siblings? Your best friends? To celebrities?

everyday

What is the bar by which you judge yourself?

-I judge by comparing that I dont have money saved, havent finished school, single 8 years

Fill in the blank: If I were *done with school* **then I would be where I want to be.**

Our culture has figured out a way for us to get "there," even if it only exists on social media.

When you think of the word *filter*, what are some of the things that come to mind? List them here.

-lies
- Fake
-pretty
-not the truth

What is your favorite Instagram filter? black & white

Or maybe your favorite Snapchat filter? with glasses

My favorite is rise. It just sounds like there's no where but up for that photo to go when you put the rise filter over it.

Our social media-driven culture has really rewired our thinking on filters. Before the days of Instagram or Snapchat, a filter had a much different definition. Now we primarily use filters on our photos to help with the lighting or in hopes that the coloring of the photo will look better.

But if I look up "filter" in the *Merriam-Webster Dictionary*, I find this definition:

"a device that is used to remove something unwanted from a liquid or gas that passes through it."[1]

Mine is the bee. It not only makes you look like a bee, but it makes you sound like a bee. And singing "Jesus Loves Me" as a bee is just awesome.

So "filter" is one word, but it can have very different definitions. The first definition is something that is applied to a picture or snap to make it look better or different than it would on it's own. It is not considered a pure form of the picture, but rather improved upon. There are even some apps (like the Mira app), which allow you to alter your face to remove flaws or change the shape of your features. When someone uses the hashtag *#nofilter*, you know that nothing was added to enhance the photo. It is what it is.

But the use of the word "filter" originated from medieval times where they used a "piece of felt through which liquid is strained."[2] Nothing was added to the liquid, but instead items were removed from the liquid.

Before K-cups became all the rage and replaced coffee pots, there was a very necessary piece of uniquely designed cloth that was placed in the upper chamber of the coffee pot. Ground coffee beans were then measured and placed in this "cloth" within the upper chamber. The cloth was known as a coffee filter. It allowed hot water to diffuse through the filter and become coffee without the grit of the bean spilling into the cup. The filter kept the beans out of the cup, but left the yummy caffeinated beverage behind to create coffee-addicts everywhere.

So, the second definition of filters would mean that something is used to remove impurities that we don't want in the end product.

WHY FILTERS?

So, why all the talk about filters? Because we apply filters and use them in our everyday lives, and they're not always social media or coffee filters.

More than any other generation before, Generation Z is constantly immersed in 24/7 news ranging from Twitter feeds, Snapchat, Instagram, and

even once in awhile Facebook (you know, so you can see what your mom or dad are posting about you). But with that constant feed comes some interesting dilemmas. Your generation can literally hear from celebrities within seconds of a tweet or a Snapchat story being sent. You can process events as they are happening with the rest of the world. This media engages humanity in virtual friendships with people and experiences they may never meet or go to. Social media has removed barriers globally and has connected us with celebrities and people that we would otherwise know very little about.

The result? We know about Taylor Swift's squad. Some of us follow her life on a daily basis. When we are soaking in those experiences, it's hard not to want that kind of life for ourselves. We want to project a life that seems like we have it all together.

And without even knowing it, we filter our lives through the lens of a celebrity on Twitter, or a group of girls that get the most likes on Insta. And those are the people we look to in order to see how our lives measure up.

KEEPING IT REAL

Let's be real here. In fact, I'm even going to place the "Keep it 100" emoji throughout this study for when I am asking you to dig deep and be honest with yourself. You know what the "Keep it 100" emoji means, right?

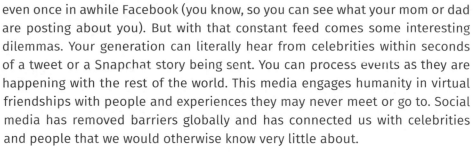

KEEP IT 100: To tell the truth, the whole truth, and nothing but the truth. AKA "keep it Real" or be honest with yourself as well as others.[3]

My pastor always says, "The first person you lie to is yourself. That's why we need to be in an accountability group—so friends can call you on it when you are not being true to yourself."

KEEP IT **What kind of filter do you use for your life (your heart, soul, mind)?**
100

Is it a social filter like in the first definition that creates a faux reality of your life? Wouldn't it be great to have some kind of filter for your heart, soul, mind that could work like a coffee filter and remove the impurities in your life?

IDENTITY IN CHRIST

We must understand who God is and His character of holiness to truly find our identity and value in Him.

Read 1 Peter 1:15-16.

15 But as the One who called you is holy, you also are to be holy in all your conduct; **16** for it is written, Be holy, because I am holy.

Underline each time you see the word "holy" mentioned in this passage.

- What are some facts that you can determine already from this passage?

- Holiness is a big deal to God, isn't it? How can you tell?

Circle the phrase that says, "the One who called you." Then write your area code above it. This part is personal.

God has something specific for you that He has tasked you with, so write your initials above the first "you."

The Greek word for "who called" is *kalesanta*. It literally means "called by name to a task."

- How does it impact you to know the Creator of the universe has called you to a task?

- The bigger question is this: Have you heard Him? Do you know that He knows you? And have you answered?

The word *holy* in this passage means "dedicated to God and set apart to the service of God." As you go about your day, imagine what it would look like to live life through this filter. A filter of knowing you are God's. You are dedicated to Him and your life's purpose is to honor and serve Him.

Let's just try this.
- How would that impact your Friday nights?
- How would that impact your friendships?
- How would that impact the shows you watch?
- How would that impact how you think about dating?
- How would that impact the dreams and goals you have for yourself?

And here's the thing that is amazing with pursuing God's holiness: As He is removing the impurities from our hearts, He is giving us His heart and making us look more and more like Him.

PURITY

Our response to the holiness of God is to reflect His character in living our lives of purity. We pursue holiness so that we might look more like Him.

So, what are some virtues that you want Him to grow in you?

What are some attributes that you long for in your heart? Use the heart drawing below to doodle those words in as a prayer for God to grow those attributes within you.

Read 1 Peter 2:9-12.

9 But you are a chosen race, a royal priesthood, a holy nation, a people for His possession, so that you may proclaim the praises of the One who called you out of darkness into His marvelous light. **10** Once you were not a people, but now you are God's people; you had not received mercy, but now you have received mercy. **11** Dear friends, I urge you as strangers and temporary residents to abstain from fleshly desires that war against you. **12** Conduct yourselves honorably among the Gentiles, so that in a case where they speak against you as those who do what is evil, they will, by observing your good works, glorify God on the day of visitation.

Underline the phrase in verse 9, "the One who called you out of darkness."

Then, write your phone number next to the word *called*. This is personal.

Draw a tombstone next to the word *darkness*.

This is where this gets real. Darkness is not just nighttime here. This means that God called His people out of death and into life with Him. He has called. Have you answered?

Without knowing Christ personally, there is no pursuit of holiness. There is no way you can be holy without God. Notice where the command comes in Scripture to abstain from fleshly desires. Is it before or after God called His people out of the darkness into magnificent light?

It's after. Because it is through Christ and Christ alone that we are able to pursue holiness and fight our fleshly desires.

Underline fleshly desires and draw a flame next to it.

List some desires below that could be good. Could those desires become bad? If so, how?

PASSIONS AND DESIRES

Desire is not a bad thing. We all have desires. It is part of who we are. We always have desires and passions for something. It could be a passion to attain admission into a certain college, or a desire for a relationship. It could also be a passion to use your gifts and talents. Very quickly there is a war that emerges out of our passions and desires.

Who will this passion and desire benefit? Is it you? Or is it God? The world is telling you to do whatever you want for your own benefit. It claims that when you do what you want, then you are free. The problem is that the world isn't the one who grants freedom. Freedom only comes through Christ.

Unfortunately, we have complicated personal holiness by trying to manage sin on our own. When constantly striving to do more good deeds than bad or attempting to overcome sin in our own strength, we are trying to be our own savior—we will always fail in this pursuit.

So as you dig into this journey of personal holiness, we will not be showing you how to manage your sin. You won't find a list of "Dos" and "Don'ts."

What you will find is a Christ-centered approach to surrendering your life—your desires, your dreams, your timeline, your plans, your relationships, your sexuality, your purity—to Christ. When you admit your need for Him, your filter changes.

The fight for purity all of a sudden is not just you alone trying to will yourself not to think certain things or look at certain images, or even determining how close to sex you will get, but it becomes a hunger for something entirely different. The hunger of your heart changes from satisfying selfish desires to seeking a relationship with the One who knows you better than you know yourself.

Some friends of mine have shared with me the battle it is for them to pursue personal holiness on their school campuses. They have said that the percentage of girls that are not sexually active is very small. As a result, their choice for personal holiness is anything but personal. It has impacted their whole campus. Thankfully, there is a group of girls that walk in this pursuit together. They encourage one another and when the struggle is real, they remind one another who they are in Christ. This group of girls has a hunger for different things. They hunger for intimacy with Christ.

Now they aren't perfect, but they are pursuing holiness as a Generation Z group of girls, just like you. You are not alone in this journey. Isn't that exciting? You will be joined by girls all over the world who will be doing this study. Take a moment to pray for the other girls discovering God's plan for their personal pursuit of holiness.

NOW WHAT?

As you consider how the truths from Scripture apply to your life, discuss these questions with your group. Be open and honest, and ask God to open your eyes to what He wants to teach you through this session.

What challenges in our culture are we up against that distract us from pursuing holiness in Christ?

Are you trying to manage your sin without Christ? Why is this dangerous?

Discuss the importance of accountability and why we all need fellow believers to help us to stay on track. Who are those people in your life?

 What are some things you need to surrender completely to Christ in order to make Him your top priority?

On your own

Find somewhere quiet and relaxing where you can spend time with God thinking about and processing what it means to live a life of holiness. Reflect on this session and what God is teaching you. Take time for some creative processing. You'll be tasked with a process and an adventure to help you think more about what you have been studying as a group.

CREATIVE PROCESS

As we close out this first session, take a moment to draw or write a response or a prayer for yourself (and for your group) in the Instagram-shaped image below as you move into this study together.

CREATIVE ADVENTURE

Use the hashtag *#filteredheart* to accompany your above creation or to share a truth that stuck with you from this session.

PRAYER

Place your hand over your heart and read this Scripture about hearts as your closing prayer:

> 23 Guard your heart above all else, for it is the source of life. 24 Don't let your mouth speak dishonestly, and don't let your lips talk deviously. 25 Let your eyes look forward; fix your gaze straight ahead. 26 Carefully consider the path for your feet, and all your ways will be established. 27 Don't turn to the right or to the left; keep your feet away from evil.
> **–PROVERBS 4:23-27**

Our Identity in Christ

GENESIS 1:26-27

26 *Then God said, "Let Us make man in Our image, according to Our likeness. They will rule the fish of the sea, the birds of the sky, the livestock, all the earth, and the creatures that crawl on the earth."*

27 *So God created man in His own image;*
He created him in the image of God;
He created them male and female.

WELCOME

You've made it through the first session! Before we begin Session 2, let's take a minute to think back to Session 1 and reflect on what we learned about being the best possible version of ourselves and how this is only possible through our Savior, Jesus Christ.

Let's begin this session on identity by getting creative. Use the space below or a page in your journal to create a collage that describes who you are to the group.

Take a moment to share with the group how you described yourself. You may have put a boyfriend's name down, you may have written the name of your family members to explain who you are, or you may have listed things you enjoy — sort of like a recipe of what you are made of. (i.e. I like this brand of clothes, I like this kind of Starbucks drink, I like this movie, I love my squad of girls and the color green.)

Press Play

Watch the video for Session 2. Think about what stood out to you most from what Amy-Jo shared, then discuss your responses to the following questions.

DISCUSS

What did you think about Amy-Jo's identity socks? List some qualities that others might use to identify you.

Amy-Jo says, "The One who made you is the One who gives you your identity." Why is it important for us to know who we are in Christ?

 KEEP IT 100 **Who or what are you putting your worth and identity in other than Christ? Journal your response here.**

Let's Talk

CULTURE

Psychologists tell us that to be able to identify and explain who you are determines the confidence and maturity that exists within you. Why is it important to know who you are?

- When you know who you are, you know who you aren't.
- When you know who you are, you know what you're worth.
- When you know who you are, you know what to build your life upon.

The problem is this, if we don't know who we are, then we may end up trying to be someone we're not, and then we have an identity problem.

MIXED MESSAGES

In today's culture, we receive a lot of messages on a daily basis from ads, social media, and even from our peers. Dove launched the Campaign for Real Beauty in 2004 with some very specific messages aimed at girls and women.

They created these mini films or short documentaries where they tried to peek into what real beauty is. This initially started as the result of some research where they found that only 4 percent of women in the U.S. felt like they could call themselves beautiful. They said that "72 percent of girls feel tremendous pressure to be beautiful."[1] So they created these films with the hope of changing those statistics. A typical *Real Beauty* campaign ad would reveal the timeline of how photos in a magazine undergo major adjustments before they ever arrive in a magazine. The ad would do a time-lapse to show how different the photo appears in the end from the original photo in the beginning.

At the same time Dove was doing their *Real Beauty* commercials, there was another product called Axe Body Spray launching an entirely different campaign. The ads typically start with a mildly unconfident young man spraying Axe body spray on himself. Then very quickly a young woman or two or several literally throw themselves at this guy in a very seductive manner just because he sprayed on this horrific-smelling cologne.

I discovered that Dove and Axe are owned by the same company. Yeah. Insert shocked emoji face here. Mixed messages for sure. Unilever is the name of the company. They are under a class-action lawsuit now because they have been selling the Real Beauty campaign and the Axe body spray campaign at the same time.

Discuss with your group how these opposing campaigns send mixed messages about our identity as girls. Journal the highlights here.

In the first ad, Dove wants girls to know that magazines aren't selling real beauty and that those images are engineered. They seem to want girls to understand that beauty looks different than what we see on the covers of magazines.

In the Axe commercial, however, girls are mere animals and cannot control themselves. Girls are not seen as a thing of beauty and worth, but rather a trophy or an accessory for this boy.

FAIRY TALES

In addition to those mixed messages, most girls have grown up listening to and watching fairy tales. These stories have threaded themselves into our culture and influenced our identity stories as girls. Let's take a look at a few of these beloved fairy tales and see what we can find out.

Let's start with Cinderella. She's kind of the queen bee of all the princesses. She finds herself in a blended family, and her step-mom and step-sisters are pretty horrible to her. I'm not going to go into all of it, but It's pretty heavy. She definitely needs some counseling. Regardless, she works hard at her chores and sings to mice and birds. One day, she receives some makeover magic and gets to go to a fancy ball. Her fairy godmother makes Cinderella look pretty for this one night. And she catches the prince's eye. Lots of things happen with some glass slippers, but we'll move on. At the end of the story, the prince rescues her from her horrible life. She gets married and lives happily ever after.

Next on the list is Ariel. She's one of my favorites because she has red hair and she's awesome. She has this amazing talent. She sings really great musical scales. Regardless of her skill, she gives up this gift (her voice) for a prince. She does get human legs in exchange, but it's kind of a bad thing in the mermaid world. She does all that to pursue a prince who she doesn't really know. Despite the evil Ursula's efforts to stop Ariel and her prince, they eventually get married and live happy ever after.

> Someone in your group might enjoy singing. If so, allow her the opportunity to sing the Ariel scales.

The last one we'll look at is Sleeping Beauty. Her life is literally on pause because she's in a magical coma. She's literally waiting for her prince to wake her up with a kiss. And no one ever mentions that she probably has really bad morning breath because she's been asleep for over a hundred years! But eventually her prince does come and find her. He kisses her. She awakes. They get married and live happily ever after.

So, we hear these stories as girls and we grow up with these fairy tales. In fact, Disney has recently continued marketing of these fairy tales into real life. They have launched an engagement ring design for each of the different princesses. Disney has woven the princess story into, "Now on your wedding day, you can be a princess and have your happily ever after."

IDENTITY IN CHRIST

Girls, your identity is not in being a fairy tale princess who lives only to find her prince. Your identity is not photoshopped. Your identity is not found in being a guy's trophy. Your identity is not even determined by you. Your identity is determined by the One who made you.

Read Genesis 1.

Note each instance you see the words "And God said or Then God said." What do you think these two phrases have to do with the way God created?

Can you find any place in Genesis 1 where it says God used a certain material or tool to create? No. So how did He do it? Let's look at how we were created.

Read Genesis 1 :26-27; 31; 2:7; 5:1-2.

Based on the above Scriptures, how did God choose to create us? Did He "voice us" into existence?

The word in Hebrew that translates into our word "created" found in Genesis 1:27 is "*bara*."[2] It means to create something from nothing. There is another Hebrew word that also translates into our word "form" that is used in Genesis 2:7. It is "*yatsar*."[3] Whereas *bara* means to create something from nothing, this type of creating that Scripture is talking about is "the forming." To form something, what do you usually use? Your hands.

Well, why are there two ways that the Scripture says we were created? Did they goof? No. When God created us in His image, we see Him use both the "*bara*" element of creating and the "*yatsar*" element of creating. So He "formed" us, but that was not enough. He breathed into us something from nothing. He breathed into us characteristics of Himself. Why is it Important to know how our Creator made us?

1. *He formed us.* God got involved with us. Even from the beginning of time, our creator desired to have a relationship with us. He got His hands "into us." He spent time shaping us and making us into something that would bring honor to His name as our Creator.

As one who was created by the Creator, how does that impact you to know He uniquely made you? He didn't just create a human manufacturing company, but He uniquely and specifically designed and formed you.

Take a moment to process how God formed you. How does that impact your identity?

2. *He breathed Inside of us something from nothing.* He made us unique when He breathed into us His Spirit.

Our identity is shaped by knowing we were made by God.

Read Genesis 1:26-27.

Circle the word "image" or "likeness" every time you see it.

> **26** Then God said, "Let Us make man in Our image, according to Our likeness. They will rule the fish of the sea, the birds of the sky, the livestock, all the earth, and the creatures that crawl on the earth." **27** So God created man in His own image; He created him in the image of God; He created them male and female. **—GENESIS 1:26-27**

IMAGO DEI

Read Genesis 5:1-2.

This is the book of the generations of Adam. When God created man, He made him in the likeness of God.

Again, circle the word "image" or "likeness."

> Whoever sheds the blood of man, by man shall his blood be shed, for God made man in his own image. **—GENESIS 9:6**

The theological term *imago Dei* means "made in the Image of God."[4] The above verses are the key verses that support that we are very special as God's creation because we are made in His likeness or image.

Does that mean that we are exact copies of God? No. Maybe a better way to explain it is that we are imagers of God on earth. We reflect some of His characteristics—mental, moral, and relational—in our beings.

Mentally, we are able to choose and reason for ourselves. Morally, we have a conscience to determine right from wrong. Relationally, we were made to be in relationship with others just like God is in relationship through the Trinity. That's God said, "Let *us* create man in *our* image." There is a social relational aspect to the Trinity.

And last, we were made to love and be loved as God is love (1 John 4:8).

This is all tied into how God made humanity. We are imagers of Him to the world. Not all bundled up in one person, but similar to how we share physical attributes with our family members, we each carry aspects or glimpses of who God is.

Do you have any physical similarities with your parents or family members? What are some of those similarities?

Well, *imago Dei* goes even deeper than physical characteristics to the very DNA of our soul. And why would God make us in His image?

PURITY

Let's dig into Scripture for the answer to why God made us in His image. We will also find out how we are supposed to honor God through our own personal holiness. Just as He is holy, we are to be holy (1 Pet. 1:16).

Read Isaiah 43:7.

"Everyone called by My name and created for My glory. I have formed him; indeed, I have made him."

Underline the phrase: "created for My glory."

God made us on purpose, in His image, and for a specific purpose. We are imagers of Him. We are designed to reflect God's glory and live for His praise.

The problem is that shortly after being created, humanity exchanged giving glory to God for giving glory to themselves or other created things. This created an identity problem for all humanity because our image has been distorted by sin.

So let's go back and see what happens after humanity was created. Adam and Eve were living in paradise. They didn't have an identity problem. They knew who they were. They were created by God. They were a creation of God. They were image bearers of God. They talked with God and had a relationship with Him.

Read Genesis 2:25.

What does Scripture say Adam and Eve felt about their appearance?

They were naked and they were not ashamed. You mean they were naked and Eve didn't ask Adam if she looked fat? She didn't cover parts of herself and say "Don't look at me?" What!? How freeing is that? Well, what happened next?

Read Genesis 3:7.

This is after Adam and Eve disobeyed God's one rule for their life in the garden of Eden.

What was the first thing they became aware of after they sinned? What was the first feeling they had once they were aware?

They were ashamed of their appearance. Once sin got in the mix, several things happened.

1. *God could not touch that which had sin in it, and so God had to separate Himself from that which He created.* Imagine the identity crisis that Adam and Eve were having. Because of this, they probably had all these new ugly feelings within them that made them feel incomplete.

Draw two stick figures and then a jagged line in between. Write the word *God* along the line to signify a torn relationship from God.

Think about what it might have been like to have a connection with your Creator, and then no longer be able to communicate with Him.

2. *Not only did sin cause separation, but it caused death to enter into the world.*

Draw a tombstone next to the stick figures with the abbreviation of RIP on it to represent the existence of death.

There were other consequences that occurred due to sin, but the one that directly impacts our topic this session is what it did to our image. Our image was marred with sin. What does that mean? It means we have an image problem.

Our image has been tainted, and now we live as a group of girls looking at our distorted image and comparing it with everyone else's distorted image. Once sin came into our image, it distorted our view of the world as well as ourselves. We lost sight of who we were designed to give glory to in the first place.

Read 1 Corinthians 13:12.

What does this verse reveal about how we see things?

Now we see things like a poor reflection in a mirror. So as we process our identity as determined by His Word—not by fairy tales, not by social media, not by other marred imagers, but by His Word—consider these questions: "Who am I?" "Do I matter?" and "Why am I here?"

If you use the spiritual coffee filter analogy and filter these questions through your new understanding of *Imago Dei*, how would you answer these three important questions?

NOW WHAT?

You are a lovely creation uniquely made by God. He loves you and shows it in the way He knit you together. You were not an accident. You were made to give glory to God even in how you were formed. God shaped you to reveal the specific gifts, creativity, personality, compassions He gave you! Unfortunately, your marred image without Jesus makes you incapable of understanding three key components.

1. *We need a Savior.* We need Jesus to make a way for us to be made right with God, to forgive our sin, and give us new life and a restored image of ourselves through Christ.

2. *If we do not have Jesus in our life, we will continue to exchange our purpose of giving glory to God with giving glory to ourselves and things.* These things will never bring satisfaction or life to us because we weren't made for that. We shortchange relationships the way God intended them to be enjoyed when we don't allow Him into the equation. We live for our glory and our gratification. We decide to do whatever we want and whatever we choose. We live a Burger King kind of life and "have it our way" all the time. We think that means ultimate freedom, but it means ultimate slavery. This is when we find ourselves addicted to whatever we allowed ourselves to try. Now it's not just a want, it's a demand.

3. *God intended us to have life with Him.* Humanity exchanged life for death. Without Christ, we have no hope of life. Without Christ, personal holiness is just a bunch of hoops we jump through that don't actually take us anywhere. Christ is the redeemer of our broken image.

Read 1 Peter 2:9-12 again.

This passage creates a "before" and "after" of our identity without Christ.

In verse 10 it says: Once we were _____ and now we are _____. Have you had that "before and after" with Jesus? Has He called you out of the darkness of a blurred image into who you really are and who He really is?

On Your Own

CREATIVE PROCESS

When you are called out of darkness by Christ, the labels we may have been wearing will no longer apply to us. We will see ourselves as Christ sees us.

Today you may identify yourself with certain labels: used, forgotten, ugly, alone, or abandoned. Ask God to search your heart and consider what your new identity is in Christ.

Then, fill in the name tag below to complete the new identity you are able to claim in Christ today.

Hello, I am

- I am set free in Christ: Romans 8:1-2
- I am secure: Romans 8:29-39
- I am dearly loved: Colossians 3:12
- I am complete: Colossians 2:9-10
- I am bought with a price: 1 Corinthians 6:20
- I am one of God's people: 1 Peter 2:9-10
- I am redeemed: Galatians 3:13
- I am forgiven: Ephesians 1:7-8
- I am strengthened by God: Philippians 4:13

CREATIVE ADVENTURE

Use **#mynewnameinChrist** and post a picture of your name tag.

PRAYER

Ask God to help you understand His character so that you can more fully understand who you are in Christ.

Forgiveness and Redemption

SESSION THREE

2 CORINTHIANS 5:17-18

17 *Therefore, if anyone is in Christ, he is a new creation; old things have passed away, and look, new things have come.* 18 *Everything is from God, who reconciled us to Himself through Christ and gave us the ministry of reconciliation...*

WELCOME

Welcome back to Session 3 of *Authentic Love*! During the last session we talked about our identity in Christ, and this week we'll talk about forgiveness and redemption. First, take a few minutes to be still and examine your heart. Is your identity rooted in Christ? If not, take some time to pray and confess anything you are putting your worth in that is not glorifying to God.

Press Play

You probably have a lot on your mind (homework, how you're going to find time for all of those required service hours, how to respond to a friend's social media post, etc.). Go ahead and write down anything you're thinking about that might be distracting. Then, get comfortable and watch the Session 3 video from Amy-Jo, taking notes and focusing on what she has to share about forgiveness and redemption in Christ.

DISCUSS

We have a need for a Restorer and a Savior. Why do we have such a deep need for forgiveness in our lives?

What are the two directions Amy-Jo mentions that we can go in our lives?

How are you pointing others to Christ through your social media posts? With your relationships?

As you look at everything you are involved in, think about your life as a case study. Are you inviting Christ into the daily moments of your life? Explain.

Let's Talk

CULTURE

Our culture is obsessed with fixing things and making things new. Can you see it in reality TV shows? One of the most recent shows that highlights this obsession is called *Fixer Upper*. It's a show on HGTV about Chip and Joanna Gaines who live in Texas. He is a contractor and she is a designer. They are married and together they help couples renovate and fix up a home that would otherwise be deemed out of style. It's fun to watch how they see potential in a home that most would give up on.

What other shows through the years can you think of that bring attention to this "fixer upper" and "make things new" trend?

Why do you think these shows are so popular? What is the general plot of one of these shows?

You can see this theme of "made like new" even in some of our favorite childhood animated films. One of my favorite animated movies is from the *Toy Story* collection. I love following the relationship of Andy and his toys. In *Toy Story 2*, Woody gets stolen because he is a collectors item and has great value, but he has to be seen by a master toy artist who remakes him to be like new.

I can see this theme when I pass the mall near my house. I sometimes see fathers lined up with their daughters outside of the American Girl store. In fact, when a doll is broken or hurt in some way, girls can actually take their dolls to the American Girl Doll Hospital. When I learned about his, I pulled up an ad for the type of services that are offered to dolls that need to be "made like new." I learned that these dolls can get an entirely new head!

I'm concerned with all that the doll is enduring at her place of residence if she needs a head replacement, but that's a completely different topic.

In this theme of "making things new" or fixing or restoring things, there is almost always a before and after story. You can even see a before and after story emerge in the American Girl Doll Hospital ad. There are the dolls that are stained and in a bad condition, and then next to it we see dolls that look brand new.

You see a before and after story emerge in home shows like *Fixer Upper* or *Extreme Home Makeover*. There's before and after pictures that show up in my Instagram feed to try and get me to buy a skincare line because "Hannah" did it and look at the results she got.

The point is, we see this theme of wanting things to be made new or fixed up all around us. The truth is that it goes deeper than our homes, our toys, or gadgets. We care about this theme at the very core of our souls. The trouble is that restoring the soul is a bit trickier than restoring our homes, our toys, or our cars. Our lives are broken and we can't fix them. We need a restorer. We need a Savior.

IDENTITY IN CHRIST

Read 2 Corinthians 5:17-18.

> **17** Therefore, if anyone is in Christ, he is a new creation; old things have passed away, and look, new things have come. **18** Everything is from God, who reconciled us to Himself through Christ and gave us the ministry of reconciliation...

The very first verse states that if Christ is in us, we are a new creation.

Circle "new creation" and write the word *new* **with sunbeams shooting off of it. Remember what kind of creation you are in Christ.**

BEFORE AND AFTER

So let's follow this theme of being made like new. Just like the before and after stories of toys and homes, if we are made new in Christ then that means that we have an "after" picture. And if we have an "after" picture that means we have a "before" picture. So what do we do with these "before and after" pictures? File them away and take them out on Sunday to remind Jesus that He's done some work on us before? No.

Let's read verses 19-21.

> **19** That is, in Christ, God was reconciling the world to Himself, not counting their trespasses against them, and He has committed the message of reconciliation to us. **20** Therefore, we are ambassadors for Christ, certain that God is appealing through us. We plead on Christ's behalf, "Be reconciled to God." **21** He made the One who did not know sin to be sin for us, so that we might become the righteousness of God in Him.

There is a word that keeps popping up in this passage that we don't use a lot in our everyday language, but it is a very important word for our everyday lives.

Circle all the instances of "reconciled" or forms of "reconciled" you see in the above passage.

Draw a little peace symbol over each word you circled to symbolize that through Christ we have found peace with God.

In verse 19, who has given us a message? What is that message?

Another way of explaining reconciliation is that we are set right with God or restored with God. So, what does that look like for us to have this message of restoration put upon us as a new creation?

Read Colossians 1:21-29 (MSG).

> You yourselves are a case study of what He does. At one time you all had your backs turned to God, thinking rebellious thoughts of Him, giving Him trouble every chance you got. But now, by giving Himself completely at the Cross, actually dying for you, Christ brought you over to God's side and put your lives together, whole and holy in His presence. You don't walk away from a gift like that! You stay grounded and steady in that bond of trust, constantly tuned in to the Message, careful not to be distracted or diverted. There is no other Message—just this one. Every creature under heaven gets this same Message. I, Paul, am a messenger of this Message.

That's a beautiful message for anyone who has acknowledged their need for a Savior. This means we have an awesome purpose now because we are walking, breathing, "Before and After" pictures to every person we meet. This message of sharing our restored "Before and After" lives is ultimately so that others can know the hope we have in Christ and so that they will have the opportunity to be restored with a purpose as well.

So to get us thinking, let's pretend that there is a physical file that we can hand to the people we meet. Spend some time journaling your answers to the following questions.

What story would your "before Christ" picture tell?

Can you remember your life without Christ? What do you remember about that life? Use this chart to list what your life was like before you knew Christ and allowed Him to restore your life. The "After" section is a space for you to list how your life is different now that you know Christ.

before | after

If you have acknowledged your need for a Savior, invited Him to be Lord of your life, and have followed through with what Romans 10:9 says, then you will be able to respond to these questions. If you do not have a relationship with Jesus Christ, then you have not experienced the restoration that comes from knowing Jesus as your Savior. My prayer is that this is something you are beginning to desire for your life. You will not be able to find restoration for your life without Christ.

PURITY

What is the difference you find in your life now with Christ?

How have you seen your relationship with Christ begin to change your purpose? Your dreams? Your desires? Your identity?

As you look at the "before and after" picture of your life, know that Satan wants to do whatever he can to destroy the "after" picture and rob God of the glory He deserves for the work He has done.

STORY OF LIFE

If you look at your life as a story, you have to acknowledge three parts to that story. First there is the protagonist. The protagonist is the hero of the story.

List some heroes of stories you are familiar with. Who would be some good examples of protagonists?

Next there is the antagonist. The antagonist is the bad guy in the story. The antagonist is trying to destroy the protagonist. There is always tension between the two.

List some examples of antagonists from stories or movies you are familiar with.

What we often don't consider in the story is the third person or persons. This person is called the agonist.

What word do you see emerge from the word *agonist*?

> If you confess with your mouth, "Jesus is Lord," and believe in your heart that God raised Him from the dead, you will be saved.
> — Romans 10:9

Agony. Yes! The agonist is caught in the middle of the battle. They often get caught in a battle they didn't choose to be in. But they feel the pain of the struggle.

That is you and me, my friend. We are the agonists. Oftentimes we think of ourselves as the hero, but that role would mean the story is all about us. And guess what? It's not.

Jesus is the protagonist. The story of the world is about Him and how He rescues us and eternally restores us to a right relationship with God forevermore.

And while we walk this earth, if we have surrendered our lives to Christ, then we have been restored and are image bearers of Christ to the world. We blare the message of Christ with our very lives and the antagonist Satan can't stand it. He can't take us away from Christ, but he can try to destroy our reputation. He can discourage us as we live our lives. He can divide us from friendships that are helpful to us. He is prowling around us like a lion trying to wound us because he knows how much our restored lives preach to a broken world.

Let's talk about ways this antagonist wounds us and our "after" pictures. Over the years, I have seen groups of students pursue holiness and chase after God's purpose in their lives. Unfortunately, I've seen some of these same students get off track and make some unwise choices to pursue their own selfish purposes. This is where Satan is ready to pounce and take their reputation and their influence for Christ in a direction they never thought was possible.

Sometimes it is a relationship that consumes them. Sometimes it is letting go of some boundaries they had in place for their purity for just one moment. Sometimes it is exchanging the pressure of shining His light in the midst of darkness for just being one of the crowd. Sometimes it is just being in the wrong place at the wrong time and someone is there to take a picture and tell their side of the story on Snapchat. And in an instant their influence for Christ doesn't look any different than the world around them.

RUINED REPUTATION

Reputations can be destroyed in an instant. Look at the example of Justine Sacco. A PR Consultant with only 170 Twitter followers, Justine jumps on a plane heading to South Africa. She tweets out one sarcastic tweet with racist overtones before the plane takes off. While her phone was off, that tweet went viral and became the number one trending tweet worldwide.[1]

When Justine finally landed in South Africa, she turned on her phone and discovered what that one tweet had done. She lost her job. Her reputation was destroyed. She suffered worldwide humiliation.

NOW WHAT?

There are two directions we can choose to live our lives. We can choose to worship God or we can choose to worship ourselves. It sounds pretty simple, but this is where the filter is helpful.

- When I am in this situation with my boyfriend, how can I invite Christ into the moment so it doesn't become a moment robbed of Christ's presence?
- When I am posting this picture on Instagram, how can I make sure the overall story is not misrepresenting who I am?
- When I tweet out this statement, is it founded in love or is it going to hurt someone?
- When I send this Snapchat to these guys, is it going to degrade who I am as a daughter of God? Am I exchanging something for popularity or to be accepted?

Maybe these are some of the situations you have found yourself in. Maybe that's where you find yourself today.

What does living with a filter look like for Christ followers who have tripped up and had our reputations ruined?

 What does it look like for daughters of God who have exchanged their purity in a moment because they thought they knew what love was, only to find out it wasn't?

I've had days where I've made choices to be funny at the expense of another person. I thought they were in on the joke, but I quickly learned how hurt they were by my teasing. In that moment I felt so humbled. I remember asking God to remind me of how He felt about me, because in that moment I didn't even like myself. I lost perspective of what my Heavenly Father thought about me. And Satan was just causing me to spiral out of control emotionally. But God is a redeeming God. He didn't leave me where I wanted to be left.

My pastor always says, "He can take the worst day of your life and make it the first line of your testimony of redemption."[2]

REDEMPTION STORY

One Sunday morning I said *yes* at the last minute to take on an assignment that normally I would have excelled in. However, in the moment I had no confidence at all in myself for anything. I stood on stage to lead a prayer time and was so nervous. Then I was merely supposed to close out the service with prayer when the live stream of the sermon went out. Everyone looked to me to take over the service and guide and direct the moment. I closed out our time together and gathered us for prayer. At the conclusion, two older men in our congregation flanked me on both sides before anyone else could get to me. They said these words: "I am proud of you."

When they said those words, I heard it in my heart, too, and I knew that my Heavenly Father was restoring my perspective of how He felt about me as His daughter.

I share that story with you to remind you that even when you find yourself drifting or tripped up from a mistake you have made, when you seek His face and repent of what you've done, God is there waiting for you to show you how much He still loves you. And He works to make you a redemption story again.

Sweet girl, if you have surrendered your life to Christ, He is your Redeemer. Not just for that day, but for a lifetime. That doesn't mean you get a license to live however you choose. It means your heart hungers more and more for the things of Christ rather than for the things of the flesh and what this world has to offer.

"We have redemption in Him through His blood, the forgiveness of our trespasses, according to the riches of His grace ..."
—Ephesians 1:7

On Your Own

CREATIVE PROCESS

Take a moment as we close out this third session to consider the gift of redemption and restoration. The Greek word for restore is *katartizo*.[3] It means to mend, order, equip, prepare, and train.

Write the word *katartizo* on your hand today as a reminder that as you go about your day, Satan will try to tell you that you are unworthy of being restored or that you aren't ready to be restored. But Christ has a different message for you.

Read 1 Peter 5:10-11.

> **10** Now the God of all grace, who called you to His eternal glory in Christ Jesus, will personally restore, establish, strengthen, and support you after you have suffered a little. **11** The dominion belongs to Him forever. Amen. **−1 PETER 5:10-11**

Christ Himself has made us a new creation and is continually restoring (mending, ordering, equipping, preparing, and training) those who have offered their lives to Him. He wants you to share your restoration story with the people around you.

CREATIVE ADVENTURE

The great hymn writer Fanny J. Crosby wrote the lyrics to "Redeemed, How I Love to Proclaim It" after she accepted Christ as her Savior. Search for the lyrics online and use these words to create a picture celebrating your redemption. Make it uniquely your own.

Use the hashtag **#redeemedstory** to share your picture.

PRAYER

Consider whether there is someone in your life who you need to seek forgiveness from. If so, take action and make amends today. Thank God for being our Redeemer and ask Him to draw you closer and closer to Him and His Word this week.

What does love look like?

1 JOHN 4:16

And we have come to know and to believe the love that God has for us. God is love, and the one who remains in love remains in God, and God remains in him.

WELCOME

Hey girls! You are halfway through this study. Way to go! We're praying for you and that God will use this study to make you more like Him. The world tells us a lot of different things about love, but we need to focus on what God's Word tells us about love. Let's dig in to what true love looks like and learn more about the author and perfecter of love.

Press Play

Watch the video for Session 4. Amy-Jo opens up by sharing a fun little love story from when she was in fourth grade. You may have had a similar experience. Listen closely, then take notes or doodle images in your journal to help you process and remember the main points from the video.

DISCUSS

This week we'll be touching on the subject of love and how true love is only found in God. Take a few minutes to respond to the following questions.

Have you ever received or given a gift that was a let-down? Share your story or journal about it here.

How does our world and culture tell us what love looks like?

What does God tell us about love? How is this different from what the world tells us about love?

Why do you think the subject of sex is not talked about much in the church? Who is the giver of sex?

Amy-Jo reminds us that God is love. Why is it important that we focus on this truth and what God's Word has to teach us about true love in our day-to-day lives?

Let's Talk

CULTURE

Love. How do you define it? People make movies about love stories. People write songs about their thoughts on it. People pen books about the romance of it. But how do we truly settle what love is?

Let's do some investigative research on what our culture says about love. Start by listening to or taking a look at the lyrics of a few of pop culture's most popular "love" songs.

What does the chorus communicate about what love looks like in a relationship?

Love through the lyrics in popular songs does not look like it cares for anyone else. It's often about the gratification of the person seeking physical touch.

What about the love song by Ed Sheeran called "Thinking Out Loud" (*X*, 2014)?

What does this song say about love? What does this song express love looks like in a relationship?

Now it's your turn. Pick a favorite love song and try to deconstruct it. What does that love song really say about love?

Our world has a lot to say about love. The problem is that not a lot of people know what love is and what love isn't. We've allowed love to take on many different meanings and become associated with many different things. Love to one person may be assigned to the way they feel about a car. Love to another person may be based on the way they feel about a person. Love to another person may relate to the way they feel when they look at a person or images of people they don't even know. Love has become this thing where people allow everyone the right to pursue it however they want to pursue it. Let's just seek freedom and let people love the way they want to love.

I was talking with some girls I mentor and asked them what it looks like to be "in love" or "in a relationship" in their school. They said that "if you are in a relationship at school, then most likely you have had sex or that is the expected thing. It's just what is done."

Think about how far that message has come from when your grandparents or great-grandparents were living. In television shows It used to be that even married couples were not allowed to have scenes where they were in the same bed. They had separate beds in movies and on TV! Sex was neither discussed nor portrayed in even married relationships on public television.

Now we have scenes featuring teenagers to married adults that portray sex as just part of a normal progressing relationship. Marriage isn't even a normal part of the progressing relationship as told via our love stories and chick flicks. Isn't it interesting how fairy tales end in marriage and our romance stories don't seem to make marriage necessary? Our world has some very different views on love, so it is important for us to see what the Bible says about love.

IDENTITY IN CHRIST

To appropriately define love we have to deconstruct its roots, like we did with the love songs earlier. So, let's look at a biblical understanding of love. We'll start by taking a closer look at these verses:

> Dear friends, let us love one another, for love comes from God.
> **–I JOHN 4:7**
>
> God's love was revealed among us in this way: God sent His One and Only Son into the world so that we might live through Him.
> **–I JOHN 4:9**
>
> Dear friends, if God loved us in this way, we also must love one another." **–I JOHN 4:11**
>
> And we have come to know and to believe the love that God has for us. God is love..." **–I JOHN 4:16A**
>
> We love because He first loved us. **–I JOHN 4:19**
>
> I give you a new commandment: love one another. Just as I have love you, you must love one another. By this all people will know that you are My disciples, if you have love for one another. **–JOHN 13:34-35**

What do these verses tell us about where love comes from?

Does the root of love come out of a selfish intent or a giving love? What is the evidence of that in these passages?

What else can you determine about love based on Scripture?

Our culture has so intertwined love with sex, so rather than trusting the world, we need to look at what the Bible says about God's design for sex. The diagram that follows on the next page will help you talk about sex and how it relates to God. In Scripture, we understand that God designed sex and gave it to us as a good gift. In Scripture, it is clearly connected to God. Our sexuality is not disconnected from Him.

How does the culture seek to distort God's good gift of love and sex?

Let's take a look at how God designed marriage to be in the beginning.

Read Genesis 2:23-25 (MSG).

I like how The Message translation paraphrases the story of Adam and Eve becoming husband and wife and celebrating their relationship the way God designed them to.

> The Man said, "Finally! Bone of my bone, flesh of my flesh! Name her Woman for she was made from Man." Therefore a man leaves his father and mother and embraces his wife. They become one flesh. The two of them, the Man and his Wife, were naked, but they felt no shame.

A GOOD GIFT

So, in light of Genesis 2:24-25, we can determine that our sexuality was designed to be connected to God. He created it and gifted it to husbands and wives.

Now the church understands scripturally that sexuality is connected to God. But as it has been communicated through the years, I feel like the message has missed the mark as far as truly knowing how to connect the gift of sex to God.

When I was a teenager, our churches seemed so worried that we'd find out that sex was good and that, within God boundaries, it is a gift, that they just skipped telling us that part and focused solely on the consequences. They would say, "Here's what you need to know: Don't do this." And they started really harping on the boundaries that God has given us and the consequences of crossing them. They said one day we'd get married and we should just wait and figure it out then. And so the problem is, oftentimes we focus on a moral checklist.

Despite our best intentions, sex got disconnected from God as a good gift simply because it wasn't talked about. Sex got connected to a moral checklist.

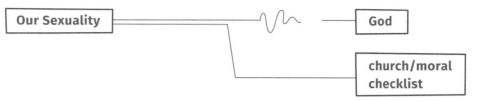

| Our Sexuality | | God |
| | | church/moral checklist |

When is it that you find your thinking drift to connecting sex to a moral checklist rather than seeing it as a gift from God?

THE DISCONNECT

And last, we have our culture. We've already talked at length regarding the varied views our culture has on love. I mean, you can just turn on the TV. In movies, and love stories, it's just natural that a person will fall in love with someone, and then they'll have sex and may or may not pursue marriage. And this cultural "love" on the big screen or TV show is not held by any boundaries. If you're not married, but you love this person, go ahead, you are free to love as you want. If you are the same gender, our culture would say go ahead and love as you want.

Culture has told us that if we disconnect our sexuality from God, we'll experience freedom. We don't need boundaries, we don't need God, we can live free. And so culture would have us erase the connection to God.

PURITY

The problem is that when we put our sexuality in our own hands, we think, *Oh yeah, I can do whatever I want with it*. And in reality, it ends up being a chain, an addiction. Something that ends up imprisoning us. Why? Because we don't understand that what God has designed for us to enjoy, within the boundaries and context of His love, is freeing. Our world doesn't understand the freedom that God offers because they don't understand true love.

Let's look at a group of people Paul sought to help understand this very thing. We'll learn about the type of love that Paul talks to them about in First Thessalonians.

To give you a little backstory on this group of people, these Thessalonians were new believers in Christ. And at the very beginning of his letter to encourage them, Paul commends them because their love had shown through in the way that they were living their lives. They were becoming known for the way they were loving each other with a brotherly love. Here's what 1 Thessalonians 1:8 says:

For the Lord's message rang out from you, not only in Macedonia and Achaia, but in every place that your faith in God has gone out. Therefore, we don't need to say anything, ...

And so, just by the way that they were living their lives, people were finding out about them. And as these new believers started discovering what it meant to pursue holy living, they started seeing some disconnects in the way they had been living. And one of the things we learn from Paul's letter is that there were certain things in that community that had been disconnected from God because it was a pagan community. They had no sexual boundaries. They did whatever they wanted, with whomever they wanted.

What is the purpose of boundaries? Why are they so important for us as believers?

The situation in Thessalonica was probably similar to some of the things we experiencing in our culture today. There were no boundaries. So when Paul was starting to speak into their lives, he had to help them understand what it looked like to reconnect their sexuality to God and why they needed to do that. He talks about the fact that there's this thing called holiness. And he begins to explain to them that as Christ followers, they are called to be set apart.

Paul pulls no punches, but simply gives them the honest truth.

Read 1 Thessalonians 4:3-8.

3 For this is God's will, your sanctification: that you abstain from sexual immorality, **4** so that each of you knows how to control his own body in sanctification and honor, **5** not with lustful desires, like the Gentiles who don't know God. **6** This means one must not transgress against and defraud his brother in this matter, because the Lord is an avenger of all these offenses, as we also previously told and warned you. **7** For God has not called us to impurity but to sanctification. **8** Therefore, the person who rejects this does not reject man, but God, who also gives you His Holy Spirit.

Paul is teaching them to begin to reconnect their sexuality to God.

Underline verse 5.

See, he acknowledges that a culture who lives disconnected from God will pursue their lustful desires the way they want because they don't know God.

Earlier we took a look at Scripture that helped us understand the root of love. We determined that love was literally God. And God's love is a giving love.

So now, looking back at the diagram on page 43, answer the following questions.

If we disconnect our sexuality from God, and God is love, then what are we truly disconnecting our sexuality from?

We are disconnecting our sexuality from true love and how God designed it. God's love is one that is giving and sacrificial.

What is the opposite of giving?

Taking is the opposite of giving and is a love that's rooted in self and selfishness. A love without God is destructive because it only serves to meet self's needs. It is not true love.

How is God's love a selfless love? Why is loving selflessly such a challenge for us?

When we understand what true love is and who true love is, then it makes sense when we read passages like 1 Corinthians 13. There is no way that we could be the kind of people that love this way unless we have Christ residing in us and transforming us with His love. God is true love.

Read 1 Corinthians 13 (ESV).

There are so many beautiful word pictures in this passage. Take some time to recreate this in your journal or on the next page with your own emojis, and think through how this passage could impact current relationships and future relationships you may have.

> **1** If I speak in the tongues of men and of angels, but have not love, I am a noisy gong or a clanging cymbal. **2** And if I have prophetic powers, and understand all mysteries and all knowledge, and if I have all faith,so as to remove mountains, but have not love, I am nothing. **3** If I give away all I have, and if I deliver up my body to be burned, but have not love, I gain nothing. **4** Love is patient and kind; love does not envy or boast; it is not arrogant **5** or rude. It does not insist on its own way; it is not irritable or resentful; **6** it does not rejoice at wrongdoing, but rejoices with the truth. **7** Love bears all things, believes all things, hopes all things, endures all things. **8** Love never ends. As for prophecies, they will pass away; as for tongues, they will cease; as for knowledge, it will pass away. **9** For we know in part and we prophesy in part, **10** but when the perfect comes, the partial will pass away. **11** When I was a child, I spoke like a child, I thought like a child, I reasoned like a child. When I became a man, I gave up childish ways. **12** For now we see in a mirror dimly, but then face to face. Now I know in part; then I shall know fully, even as I have been fully known. **13** So now faith, hope, and love abide, these three; but the greatest of these is love. **(ESV)**

NOW WHAT?

Girls, as we conclude this session on love, I pray that you understand that true love has already found you. What God has already given to you cannot be topped by a guy.

Determine now what kind of love you are pursuing. A love that is a giving love and is connected to God, or a false sort of love that may seem like it is true, but in reality falls short and leads to disappointment, frustration, addiction. This last kind of love falls short every time.

When you find a friendship with a guy that is based on God's love, then the focus shouldn't center around physical touch or sex. You should begin to find enjoyment in shared experiences and learning about how God is at work in each other. Then you begin to celebrate each other and remember to focus your affection on the originator of love, you'll find out what it looks like to see true love at work in your relationships.

On Your Own

CREATIVE PROCESS

Take your 1 Corinthians emojis and post this passage on a bathroom mirror you use every day. Remind yourself that you have already found true love in the One who is love—God. When you wake up as one who is loved and not searching to be loved, that should change your whole pursuit for the day!

CREATIVE ADVENTURE

Use the hashtag **#Godislove** and share how that truth and what you have learned this session impacts you. You can also snap a photo of 1 Corinthians 13 and share how it impacts your identity as one who is loved by God.

PRAYER

Pray specifically that God would guard and protect your heart and that He would guide you to make wise decisions regarding your friendships and relationships.

If your view of love has been distorted by what our culture says love looks like, ask God to help redefine your view of love according to His Word.

What is humility?

ISAIAH 66:1-2

1 *This is what the LORD says: Heaven is My throne, and earth is My footstool. What house could you possibly build for Me? And what place could be My home?* 2 *My hand made all these things, and so they all came into being. This is the LORD's declaration. I will look favorably on this kind of person: one who is humble, submissive in spirit, and trembles at My word.*

WELCOME

Girls, thank you for being a part of this study! I hope you've had time to reflect on God's love for you and how that shapes our purity and how we are called to live lives of holiness. This week we'll be looking at something that hits to the core of our hearts. We are going to learn about humility and how God is the only One who should be on the throne.

Press Play

Watch the Session 5 video and pay close attention to what Amy-Jo has to share with us about the humblebrag and the humblebrag birthday post on social media.

DISCUSS

Share openly with your group this week, or if you prefer, share one-on-one with an accountability partner or mentor.

 Are you obsessed with being the star of your own story? Think about and share how this is evident on social media.

Amy-Jo says, "Humility is the opposite of pride." Consider and journal about how pride is sneaking into your own life.

Do you tend to plan and take ownership of your life without seeking God's best? How so?

What does Revelation 4 say we'll do with our crowns at the end of the story?

Pray together in small groups as you prepare to dig into Scripture. Ask God to reveal any pride in your life and to clothe you in humility at the start of each day.

CULTURE

I keep most of the encouraging handwritten notes, letters, and cards that people send me. It's just something I've done since I was little. I have little notes hidden in various pockets in my backpack so when I'm digging for something, I'll inevitably find one and immediately be cheered up. In my office, I have a box of notes I have kept from middle school on. It's been a source of great joy, as the notes document the awkwardness that was my life during that time. I kept "love notes" and "friend notes" that nowadays would not exist due to text messaging. These handwritten notes are some of the best. Here's one note I received from a boy who was trying to ask me out, but ended up flattering himself more than he did me.

> "Amy-Jo, Hello, how's everything going? Things are pretty cool here. So, how is everything? You haven't talked to me much this year. I guess I wrote this note to you because I was interested in some things. First of all I know in the years past, you have liked me and we just have stayed as friends. I know sometimes you had to wait behind Jenny and Mindy. I was just wondering if that was true. I also wanted to know if you like me now? I'm just wondering because if you do, I guess you really must like me and care about me. I know I care about you even though sometimes I can't express it."

Poor guy! He didn't quite know how to flatter a girl, did he? Let's blame this on the fact that he was in middle school when he wrote it. He grew up to be a caring individual, but in his early days he definitely did not exhibit humility.

Humility is an interesting attribute. You really can't claim you have humility because then you're not being humble. What does humility really even mean?

One definition is this:

hu·mil·i·ty (noun)

a modest or low view of one's own importance; humbleness[1]

Synonyms:
1. lack of pride, lack of vanity;
2. servility, submissiveness[2]

Number 2 is a pretty accurate description of what humility is. And we don't see a lot of that in our culture. In fact, it's quite the opposite.

There's even a term called a humblebrag. Do you know what this is?

hum·ble·brag (noun)

a statement on social media in which you pretend to be modest but which you are really using as a way of telling people about your success or achievements[3]

You see humblebrags all the time on social media. My favorite place to see a humblebrag is on Instagram.

HUMBLEBRAG BIRTHDAY GRAM

The best time to spot a humblebrag is on a friend's birthday. Everyone wants to wish their friend a happy birthday, but a humblebrag birthday gram is where you post the best picture of you next to an okay picture of the birthday person you are celebrating.

Imagine a girl who is wishing her friend a happy birthday. Her friend's birthday is denoted by the tag. In fact, the girl who is being celebrated doesn't even have her face showing. Her hair is in her face! But the girl who posted the photo is looking perfectly sweet. This picture celebrates the friend who posted the photo, not the birthday girl. While it may be a fun picture, it is a humblebrag birthday gram. Sweet friends for sure.

We post beautiful pictures of ourselves with the guise of celebrating our birthday friend. The problem is, the birthday friend may not like the photo you chose of her. But it seems like that's not the objective of a humblebrag birthday gram.

Can you think of a time when you may have found yourself participating in a humblebrag? Have you ever posted a humblebrag on Instagram or Snapchat? Share about it.

What's the best humblebrag post you have seen on social media?

It's okay to admit. It is tempting for us all. You can even come clean and make a vow now to do everything you can to stay clear from the humblebrag web of vanity.

In all seriousness, social media has clearly amped up our love for ourselves. We have become obsessed with letting people know what we're eating, what we're doing, and who we are with. It truly can twist reality for us and make us think that we are the star of our life.

IDENTITY IN CHRIST

We forget that this whole thing called life is not about us. And forgetting that impacts everything.

Let's take a look at Isaiah 66:1-2.

1 This is what the LORD says: Heaven is My throne, and earth is My footstool. What house could you possibly build for Me? And what place could be My home? **2** My hand made all these things, and so they all came into being. This is the LORD's declaration. I will look favorably on this kind of person: one who is humble, submissive in spirit, and trembles at My word.

Okay doodlers (me included), there is too much imagery in verse 1 to not be doodled. So use the space above to sketch to your heart's content what verse 1 could look like if you were tasked with providing an illustration.

What do you take away about how big God is by what He says in these verses?

Why do you think God is reminding us about His authority and His greatness here?

In doing so, what do we determine about our rank or authority?

Tonight before I was getting ready to write this session, I was talking on the phone with my brother who lives a great distance away. While we were talking, my 4-year-old son decided to stack the patio cushions up as high as he could and then stack other odds and ends as well. As I was watching him build, I never thought he might actually climb this tower of terror. However, as I finished my call, I saw to my dismay that he was ascending this boy-made mountain. Before I could snatch him up, he stepped up and declared, "I am king!" and literally within seconds he had fallen off the collapsing cushions, scraped his knees, and was in tears as I picked him up and consoled him. The saying "Pride comes before the fall" literally flashed through my mind.

How often are we like this before our Maker?

Consider how prideful we must be as humans to suggest to the One who created everything that we could make Him a place to live in. Also think about how prideful we must be to suggest to the One who is in control of everything that we know what's best for our lives.

Think about the throne image. List some things that you have declared yourself to be in control of rather than submitting to God.

It happens to all of us. There is a battle going on within our hearts that revolves around the word *lordship*. When we say that Jesus is our Lord and Savior, I honestly believe that we focus more on what Christ did to save us than the surrender necessary to making Him King of our hearts and lives.

The Lord desires humility in the hearts of His children because humility means we have a right understanding of who God is and who He is not. This was the battle that was going on in the garden. Eve wanted to be like God. She was like my son who decided to climb the tower to proclaim, "I am King!" Very quickly she found herself broken and aware of how not in control she was. She had been deceived.

The people who sit on earthly thrones typically wear crowns or tiaras on their heads. Crowns and tiaras denote royalty and authority here on earth. Check out what happens to our crowns in heaven.

Read Revelation 4:10b-11.

> **10B** "They cast their crowns before the throne, saying, **11** 'Worthy are you, our Lord and God, to receive glory and honor and power, for you created all things, and by your will they existed and were created.' **(ESV)**

We make our own crowns here on earth, don't we? Oftentimes in things we find our identity, significance, and purpose in other than Christ.

What would it look like if we actually laid those "crowns" that we cling to at the feet of Christ on this side of heaven? What would it take for us to "toss our tiaras"?

From the pages of God's story, it looks a lot like acknowledging that He is God and we are not. It is only because of Him that we can live lives of purity and personal holiness.

PURITY

You may be asking yourself: *What does humility have to do with my personal holiness?* Great question.

When the prophet Isaiah came face-to-face with the glory of God in the temple, he cried out these words.

Read Isaiah 6:5.

"My destruction is sealed, for I am a sinful man." (NLT)

Isaiah's first response when confronted with the holiness of God was *I'm going to die because I am a sinner.*

Do you see the connection with humility and seeing sin in our lives?

Humility is having a right view of who we are before God and others. Pride is having a wrong view of who we are before God and others.

What is a right understanding of our own humility? It is when we recognize that He is God and we are not. And what is a wrong reality exhibited in pride? Pride is when we have begun to elevate ourselves above God and others.

KING DAVID

The story of King David is a great way for us to understand how this battle between humility and pride shows up. King David's pride deeply impacted his heart and his personal holiness.

Read 2 Samuel 11.

Verse 1 is a very important verse because it tells us something about King David that we can't overlook.

> **1** In the spring when kings march out [to war], David sent Joab with his officers and all Israel. They destroyed the Ammonites and besieged Rabbah, but David remained in Jerusalem.

King David was not doing what kings routinely did. He sent everyone else out to war, but he must have felt entitled to a break. It was during this break that he began to not only become entitled to rest, but we see in verse 2 that he began to feel entitled to Bathsheba, another man's wife.

> **2** One evening David got up from his bed and strolled around on the roof of the palace. From the roof he saw a woman bathing—a very beautiful woman.

Let's remember something about King David—he was not where he was supposed to be at this moment. And in his staycation, he had nothing to do but take a stroll. You can see the erosion of his personal holiness in the next few verses.

> **3** So David sent someone to inquire about her, and he reported, "This is Bathsheba, daughter of Eliam and wife of Uriah the Hittite."

At this point David had heard not only a name, but also that she was a person. She was someone's daughter and someone's wife. King David should have stopped when he heard this report. But pride tells you that you are entitled to do what you want and that you are in control. So . . .

> **4** David sent messengers to get her, and when she came to him, he slept with her. Now she had just been purifying herself from her uncleanness. Afterward, she returned home. **5** The woman conceived and sent word to inform David: "I am pregnant."

Now notice that Bathsheba no longer has a name. Here she is referenced indirectly just as something that King David feels entitled to. And the rest of the story we see King David trying to cover up the mistakes he made.

Then, verse 27b sums up what happens when we sit on the throne instead of God.

"However, the LORD considered what David had done to be evil."

Underline all the ways we know Bathsheba is being talked about without her name ever appearing (i.e. her, she, etc.)

Now read Psalm 51.

This was King David's response soon after the prophet Nathan confronted King David with his sin.

Do you see the humility in David? He was confronted with his sin and he was broken before God. His pride had been removed and he had a right understanding of who God is and who he was before God.

See if you can find the three parts of his prayer to God in Psalm 51.

1. He verbally confesses his sin.
2. He prays for forgiveness and cleansing of his sin.
3. He prays for his relationship with God to be restored.

"The sacrifice pleasing to God is a broken spirit, God, You will not despise a broken and humbled heart." –PSALM 51:17

What a beautiful prayer to God out of a humbled heart.

NOW WHAT?

Girls, as you consider the story of King David, can you see how pride can cause you to be blind to how you may be choosing to live your life and how you may be living in opposition to God's desire for your life?

If you have areas in your heart that you have been seeking to fill with people, places, or things other than God, don't leave this moment without coming before Him and exchanging your pride for a humble heart.

Read Colossians 3:12.

"Therefore, as God's chosen people, holy and dearly loved, clothe yourselves with compassion, kindness, humility, gentleness, and patience." (NIV)

See, this is the top of the line in the outfits that you should be eyeing every morning before you are finished getting ready for the day ahead. Clothing ourselves with these things begins with the posture of our hearts before God. Come before Him in prayer and ask Him to clothe you with compassion, kindness, humility, gentleness, and patience. Thank Him for choosing you and for loving you, and seek to honor Him with how your life each and every day.

On Your Own

CREATIVE PROCESS

Re-read Psalm 51 and highlight one of the passages that sticks out to you. Then use this space to visually recreate that passage into a picture using words or images.

CREATIVE ADVENTURE

Today's creative adventure is to share your creation on social media or with a friend. Use the hashtag **#realhumility.**

PRAYER

Begin this time by going somewhere quiet where you will not have interruptions. If you are able to, consider observing a posture of humility (bowing or kneeling) as you pray. Ask God to help you put on humility each and every day (Col. 3:12). Make it a habit and priority to pray for the needs of others. It is easy to tell someone you are praying for them, but really seek to take the time to pray for others in your life and those who might not yet know the Lord as their Savior.

Surrender to Self-Sacrifice

SESSION SIX

ROMANS 12:1

Therefore, brothers, by the mercies of God, I urge you to present your bodies as a living sacrifice, holy and pleasing to God; this is your spiritual worship.

WELCOME

Girls, we only have two weeks to go! Thanks for sticking with it and truly committing to our time together. Last session we discussed humility and how we like to be in control, but God is ultimately on the throne. This session we'll look at how we are to put Christ first, which affects all areas of our lives, and specifically how we are to offer our bodies as living sacrifices (Rom. 12:1).

Press Play

Get settled and comfortable, then watch the Session 6 video as a group. Take notes here or in your journal as you watch.

DISCUSS

Put aside any distractions and focus on the questions that follow. Discuss what Amy-Jo shared about self-sacrifice and how Christ is the ultimate example.

In the story from the 2016 Olympics, what did Abbey sacrifice to help Nikki?

How does Christ's self-sacriifice call us to sacrifice for His kingdom and His glory?

What does the word "Christian" mean?

What does self-sacrifice mean when it comes to purity? Why is it worth it for us to say *no* to certain things as we seek to live in holiness?

Consider and pray about what God might want you to surrender as you seek to bring honor and glory to Him.

Let's Talk

CULTURE

There are a lot of sporting competitions that are fun to watch, but of them all the Olympics is my favorite. It's not only watching the athletes compete that's exciting, but the competition mashed with the backstory of these athletes makes me root even harder during the games.

PURPOSE

One of the campaigns that was launched prior to the 2016 summer Olympics was an ad for Under Armour featuring Michael Phelps. It's a documentary mashup of the day-in and day-out routine that Phelps put his body through to be ready for his final Olympics. And as Phelps' story began to emerge, we learn that for over a decade he had struggled with substance abuse. He had even contemplated taking his own life in 2014. But that was when a friend, who was a Christ-follower, confronted him with good news and handed him a book titled *The Purpose Driven Life*. Soon after Phelps' checked himself into rehab, God got a hold of his life and Phelps began to understand his purpose. Under Armour ends the documentary with Phelps emerging from early morning and late night workouts to stand in the light with applause. The slogan flashes across the screen: *It's what you do in the dark that puts you in the light.*

And that is just one of the many stories that emerged from the 2016 Olympics documenting the immense physical sacrifice required to mentally and physically prepare to compete in the Olympics.

We only see an athlete compete for a few seconds or minutes and then see them awarded the medals. Under Armour's ad campaign, however, reminded us that those seconds and minutes are the result of years and years of dedication and sacrifice.

SELF-SACRIFICE IN THE OLYMPICS

Another amazing story of sacrifice came out of the games in Rio when Nikki Hamblin from New Zealand and Abbey D'Agostino from the U.S. were competing in the women's semi-final 5000 meter race. The official report from The Olympic website said this: "New Zealand runner Nikki Hamblin tripped and fell to the ground during the 5,000m race, accidentally bringing American D'Agostino down behind her with around 2,000m to go. The 24-year-old D'Agostino was quick to get up again, yet instead of carrying on with her race she stopped to help the stricken Hamblin to her feet, encouraging her to join her in attempting to finish the race. However, during her tumble, D'Agostino suffered an ankle injury, slowing the runner down, but Hamblin sportingly hung back to, in return, offer her encouragements. The two women went on to complete the race together."[1]

They both were awarded a very rare award called The Fair Play Trophy, which has only been awarded 17 times in history. When asked about the story, Abbey D'Agostino credited her faith in God for causing her heart to react to Nikki in that way.

What a sacrifice both runners made for each other! And what a testimony to God! Abbey said this later: "Although my actions were instinctual at that moment, the only way I can and have rationalized it is that God prepared my heart to respond that way. This whole time here, He's made clear to me that my experience in Rio was going to be about more than my race performance — and as soon as Nikki got up I knew that was it."[2]

Sacrifice is an important part of pursuing personal holiness. And similar to Olympic athletes training to compete in the Olympic games, sacrifice is not something that happens overnight. It is a journey that we must continue on every day, trusting God to guide us and looking to Him for the strength live for His glory.

Sacrifice will show up in the Christian life. It shouldn't surprise us that we would find ourselves at some point or often sacrificing our wants and desires to make room for God's wants and desires. The word *Christian* was mockingly assigned to early Christ followers because it meant "little Christs." But believers considered it a name of honor and continued calling themselves Christians.

IDENTITY IN CHRIST

Read Acts 11:26 to see where Christ's followers originally were named Christians.

I share this with you because as "little Christs" we are called to look more like Christ than the world. And Christ Himself gave the ultimate sacrifice in giving His life for you and me. So if we are "little Christs," then yes we will surely see sacrifice show up in our lives.

A LIVING SACRIFICE

In fact, Paul shares with us these verses from Romans 12:1-2.

> **1** Therefore, brothers, by the mercies of God, I urge you to present your bodies as a living sacrifice, holy and pleasing to God; this is your spiritual worship. **2** Do not be conformed to this age, but be transformed by the renewing of your mind, so that you may discern what is the good, pleasing, and perfect will of God.

I like how Romans 12:1-2 is paraphrased in The Message:

> So here's what I want you to do, God helping you: Take your everyday, ordinary life—your sleeping, eating, going-to-work, and walking-around life—and place it before God as an offering. Embracing what God does for you is the best thing you can do for him. Don't become so well-adjusted to your culture that you fit into it without even thinking. Instead, fix your attention on God. You'll be changed from the inside out. Readily recognize what he wants from you, and quickly respond to it. Unlike the culture around you, always dragging you down to its level of immaturity, God brings the best out of you, develops well-formed maturity in you.

Sacrifice is an every day thing.

Underline the words "living sacrifice" and draw your very best emoji of a heartbeat line like you would see in a hospital to monitor your vitals.

Sacrifices didn't stay alive in the Old Testament era. God's people would lay their sacrifices on the altar as a way to ask for forgiveness of their sins. The death of that animal was a reminder that the payment of sin was death.

As Christ offered His life as the ultimate sacrifice for you and me, we no longer have to offer sacrifices of dead animals for our sins. Christ lives within us as Christ followers, and Paul reminds us that now we offer ourselves as *living* sacrifices. That's the reason you have a heartbeat line over the living sacrifice. You are alive in Christ!

A pastor friend and I were talking about this passage one day and he said something that forever changed my understanding of this verse. He casually mentioned that a dead sacrifice never gets up from the altar, but a living sacrifice can lay down and make a decision the next day to climb off the altar.

That is the struggle of the pursuit of holiness. We struggle daily to be a living sacrifice that keeps our life on the altar.

> We are to surrender our lives daily to Christ.

RUTH'S GENEALOGY TO JESUS

One of my favorite Bible stories is that of Ruth. Ruth had no idea that a man named Boaz would be a part of her future. She had married a man who was the son of Naomi, and due to famine Ruth's husband, brother-in-law, and father-in-law died. Their deaths left these three women in a terrible situation. Women in Ruth's day did not enjoy the same rights women have today. Women at this time relied upon their husbands to speak for them and help provide basic needs for survival. Without a man in the picture, their future was grim.

Read Ruth 1.

What decision is Ruth faced with? And what does she decide?

With this decision, what sacrifices has she made? Why do you think she made those sacrifices?

Not to spoil a good love story, but Ruth, who had turned her back on the gods of her country to follow after Naomi's God and make Him Lord of her life, had seen God's faithfulness in providing for her. Boaz ended up being the man that married Ruth and took care of Naomi as well. My favorite part of the story is the ending.

Read Ruth 4:13-17.

13 Boaz took Ruth and she became his wife. When he was intimate with her, the LORD enabled her to conceive, and she gave birth to a son. **14** Then the women said to Naomi, "Praise the LORD, who has not left you without a family redeemer today. May his name become well known in Israel. **15** He will renew your life and sustain you in your old age. Indeed, your daughter-in-law, who loves you and is better to you than seven sons, has given birth to him." **16** Naomi took the child, placed him on her lap, and took care of him. **17** The neighbor women said, "A son has been born to Naomi," and they named him Obed. He was the father of Jesse, the father of David.

Now read Matthew 1:1-17. In Matthew 1:5-6 you should see some familiar names.

Who is mentioned in that verse?

Read Matthew 1:17. Who do we find at the end of the lineage?

God was all over this story of Ruth, wasn't He? Ruth wasn't the star of the story. She sacrificed her future to go with her mother-in-law, and in doing so found herself right in the middle of God's plan for her life. No one could have told her that she would have been written into the genealogy of the Messiah.

You never know what God will do with our daily acts of sacrifice. We simply ask Christ to help us look more like Him and pursue His wants and desires each day more than we pursue our own wants and desires.

How might sacrifice look different in different seasons of your life?

What does daily sacrifice look like for you now?

What area of your life do you need to surrender to God's will and His plan?

In each of these scenarios, sacrifice looks like living for God and not living for self.

When I was a little girl, one day I was given a red autograph book by my Sunday school teacher. There were some missionaries speaking at our church that day, and my teacher urged me to get their autographs.

I was extremely shy, but that is exactly what I did with that autograph book once I heard these missionaries share their testimony of God working through them in the areas they were assigned to serve. And I didn't stop there. I kept using that little autograph book for many years. Now it has hundreds of autographs of missionaries. I began a love of missionary stories that has lasted throughout my life.

PURITY

ELISABETH ELLIOT

I absolutely love missionary biographies that tell how God called them to leave what they were doing and go to where He was sending them.

One is the story of Elisabeth Elliot. Elisabeth and her husband, Jim, had a beautiful love story that was documented in a book Elisabeth later wrote titled *Passion and Purity*. In that book she shares that as she pursued Christ, her heart was also becoming aware of this man, Jim, whom she would later marry.

She wrote such statements as: "When obedience to God contradicts what I think will give me pleasure, let me ask myself if I love Him."[3]

In this statement you can see the battle for God's wants versus her own wants. And as she continuously laid that relationship before God, He called Jim and Elisabeth to marry and serve together as international missionaries to Ecuador.

They had a 10-month-old daughter and had been married for four years when Jim and four other men who had been trying to reach out to the Auca tribe attempted to make physical contact with tribe members. The five men were later discovered to have been killed.

Elisabeth, with her 10-month-old daughter, continued to work alongside of Rachel Saint who was the sister of one of the five men killed.

While serving in Ecuador, the people gave Elisabeth the tribal name *Gikari*, meaning "Woodpecker."

SELFLESS SACRIFICE

It was through the work of these women and their ability to forgive the murderers of these five men that God moved in the tribe of Auca Indians, who eventually came to know the love of Christ.

This was not an overnight decision for Elisabeth to choose to do this with her life. She had begun choosing to lay her life down before Christ long before this path was even known to her.

How do you see sacrifice shown in the life of Elisabeth Elliott?

As I researched Elisabeth Elliott's life, I stumbled upon a video from her memorial service from 2015. It was a beautiful tribute to a life well lived for God.

Her best friend shared that Elisabeth told her in the midst of all that was going on and after Jim had been killed that she cried out to God, wondering why she was there in the jungle. It was in the passage of Isaiah 43:10 that Elisabeth shared about what God reminded her.

Read Isaiah 43:10.

> "You are My witnesses"— this is the LORD's declaration—"and My servant whom I have chosen, so that you may know and believe Me and understand that I am He. No god was formed before Me, and there will be none after Me."

Elisabeth Elliot said that this became her pursuit. She needed to know more about the character of her God so that she would not be shaken in the midst of life's trials. And that pursuit ended up blessing an amazing amount of people as she shared what she learned about God.

NOW WHAT?

Read 1 Corinthians 6:20.

"... for you were bought at a price. Therefore glorify God in your body."

What is the "price" that this passage is referring to?

How can you glorify God with your life in your relationships and by how you treat others? How can you glorify Him by what you share and post on social media?

During the first century in Galilee, a wedding between a woman and a man involved a longer process than we are familiar with today. When a woman was ready to marry, her father and the father of the man she wanted to marry had to decide on a bride price. This was to compensate the bride's family for her loss. Now remember that women were seen as property, so their price was based on the work they could bring to the family. To lose your daughter to marriage came with an emotional and physical cost.

This passage reminds us that Jesus has paid the price with His own blood, His life as He laid it down sacrificially for us—the church—His Bride.

So as we make the decision to sacrifice our lives daily, we remember that this life is not our own. He is God and we are not. And as we see the story unfold of how God works in and through us, we will be amazed at the adventure of sacrifice and what that looks like from season to season.

On Your Own

CREATIVE PROCESS

Your creative process today is to read the lyrics to "I Surrender" by All Sons & Daughters (*Poets & Saints*, 2016). A quick search on the Internet should pull it up. Then print a copy or journal it down. Circle the lyrics that most resonate with you after this study on sacrifice.

CREATIVE ADVENTURE

Your creative adventure today is to share something you've learned from this study on sacrifice via your social media channel. What does sacrifice look like for you?

Use the hashtag ***#livingsacrifice*** to share with others on social media.

PRAYER

Ask God to open your eyes to what area of your life you need to surrender to His control. If there is any area you are holding back from Him, confess this now. Praise Him for His goodness and grace, and pray that He would reveal to you how you can sacrifice your time, money, or abilities in order to serve others this week.

Running the Race

1 CORINTHIANS 9:24

Don't you know that the runners in a stadium all race, but only one receives the prize? I'm begging you to run in such a way to win the prize.

WELCOME

So glad you are back, girls! Last session we talked about how we are to offer our bodies as living sacrifices and how this means that sometimes we have to surrender our own plans and priorities. In this session we'll talk about endurance and what it means to run the race

Press Play

Get comfy and settled, then watch the Session 7 video as a group. Amy-Jo shares her half-marathon experience with us and encourages us to endure in our walk with the Lord. Ultimately, our focus must be on Christ. His Word reveals how we are to endure through the joys as well as the difficulties.

DISCUSS

What are the two gadgets Amy-Jo mentions that are in her office? Do they still work? How is this different from some recent clothing lines that are designed to fall apart?

Who does endurance belong to? Why is this important for us to understand?

Amy-Jo says, "Our daily walk with God impacts our daily endurance." How should this affect how we walk with God each day?

Why is accountability and encouragement from others so important as we journey with Christ? What does your "team" look like?

Let's Talk

CULTURE

Lately there seems to be a fascination with vintage finds. Generation Z is all about nostalgia. This is why polaroid cameras are back in style and vintage record players are being bought up from thrift stores.

In my office, I have a classic Nintendo Entertainment System complete with controllers and cartridges hooked up to an old TV just for those moments when I need to play an old game of Super Mario Brothers.

I also have an old typewriter that my mother gave me from when she was a teenager. It doesn't even have electricity, and it still is in pretty good condition. The first question that I usually get when people see my typewriter or my Nintendo is: *Does it still work?*

These gadgets have endured several decades, and it is fascinating to see them still at work in this present time. The endurance of an object has a lot to do with the material that the object is made of. Did you know that even recently it has been determined that some clothing manufacturers do not make their clothes to endure the test of time, let alone a year. They are intentionally designed to fall apart.

And as much as I love some Swedish named furniture, it's unlikely that IKEA will ever be found in an antique store. You just know when you buy it that it's made with material that likely won't last very long.

What is one thing in your house right now that has truly endured the test of time? Draw a picture of it here.

Why do you think it has endured? Does its endurance make it more or less valuable?

What is a definition of endurance anyway?

en·dur·ance (noun)

The fact or power of enduring an unpleasant or difficult process or situation without giving way.

IDENTITY IN CHRIST

Endurance in the life of a Christian is something that is beautiful to watch and nothing that the individual can take credit for. What do I mean when I say that?

Read 2 Thessalonians 3:5.

"May the Lord direct your hearts to God's love and Christ's endurance."

Paul understood that it wasn't the endurance of believers that he had confidence in, but their God.

Underline "God's" and "Christ's" in this passage.

The "s" found at the end of God and Christ shows possession—the love of God and the endurance of Christ. Why is that so important to note?

This life that Christ has called us to is not to be lived in our own strength. If we do that, we will have as much endurance as the clothing that we buy these days. We don't have the material on our own to endure all that we will face in this world. But Christ has overcome and He is victoriously living within those of us that are Christ followers. It's through His endurance that we find our ability to endure temptations, trials, circumstances out of our control, and the battles of the flesh.

Let's look at a few character studies of those who have gone before us and have modeled endurance.

JOSEPH

The first person we're going to look at is Joseph. Now the passage we are going to read regarding Joseph's life starts somewhat in the middle. At this point in his life, Joseph had already been sold into slavery by his brothers and he found himself in a pagan land. Let's see what happened in the midst of the continuing saga of Joseph.

Read Genesis 39:1-6.

What do you learn about Joseph from this account?

What do you learn about Joseph's faith in God?

Remember that he was living as a man of God in a pagan country. Egyptians did not believe in Joseph's God. But from this account, Joseph lived his life in such a way that his daily life called attention to his spiritual walk with the Lord.

> Read Genesis 39:7-10.

What do we learn about Joseph's walk with the Lord in the face of temptation?

What key things did Joseph do when he was tempted daily by his boss' wife?

What was the final thing Joseph did to resist temptation?

Joseph's walk with God characterized every part of his life. His work ethic was characterized by his walk with God. His ability to flee temptation and respond in a God-honoring way was characterized by his walk with God. He endured because he walked with God daily.

Joseph knew he was under attack. He did everything in his power to continue doing his job rather than focus on the temptation he was facing. He would ignore the wife. He would remove himself from her presence. Eventually, he literally ran away from the temptation.

One aspect of endurance in terms of our personal holiness is ensuring that we invite Christ into our daily plan of protection from temptations that may trip us up.

PLAN OF ACTION

"And lead us not into temptation, but deliver us from the evil one." –Matthew 6:13 (NIV)

I don't know about you, but I have a plan of action in case there is a break-in, fire, or hostage situation at my home. I have never experienced a break-in, fire, or hostage situation so it would be easy for me to say I'm not a target. Regardless, I have a service added to my home that offers protection in such situations—it automatically sends a response team to rescue my family should they be notified of one of the above scenarios. The catch is that I have to turn on the alarm each day to activate this protection. If I do not turn on the alarm, I do not receive the protection. I must then rely on my ninja skills to protect me, which turns out are not very good. The truth is that if I ignore the daily task of turning on the alarm, I am open to attacks on my home. The same is true for our lives.

Matthew 6:13 is a prayer to call out to God for protection against scenarios we could not manage on our own. And not only protection, but salvation from these evil schemes which set out to snare us every day.

"And lead us not into temptation, but deliver us from the evil one."
–MATTHEW 6:13 (NIV)

Upon first hearing this prayer, the listener might misunderstand why we must pray to God to keep us from temptation and evil. Is God not good? Does He dangle us as bait to the evil one? As I pondered these questions through my study, I was elated to know that this is not a prayer pleading with God not to take us toward temptation, but rather a prayer confessing our weakness in getting distracted by our human desires. The prayer is inviting God to enter into the equation of our lives.

This prayer reminds us that we are not able to do this life on our own. We need Christ to lead and deliver us. He has once and for all taken care of our sin problem, but each day we have this tendency to flirt and hang out with temptations that Satan uses to snare us.

DANIEL

The next story we're going to look at is a story of four God-fearing young guys who found themselves taken from their home against their will to live in a pagan society. These four friends have a few documented moments in the Book of Daniel that I want us to look at as we learn about the endurance of their faith.

Read Daniel 1:3-21.

Summarize the story that we see in Daniel 1:3-21.

What do we learn about Daniel and his friend's walk with God in this passage?

Some commentaries suggest that Daniel and his friends decided not to eat the food due to the command in Exodus 34:15-16.

> **15** "Do not make a treaty with the inhabitants of the land, or else when they prostitute themselves with their gods and sacrifice to their gods, they will invite you, and you will eat their sacrifices. **16** Then you will take some of their daughters as brides for your sons. Their daughters will prostitute themselves with their gods and cause your sons to prostitute themselves with their gods.

Regardless of whether the food was sacrificed to idols or not, it was still not prepared in accordance with how God had commanded the Hebrews to prepare their food. Daniel exhibited a courageous faith in desiring to please God in all he did, even in a culture that did not know about God's laws.

Let's follow the friends into another situation where their identity was so woven into their DNA that they were able to withstand the king's command when it went against their faith in God.

Read Daniel 1:7 to get acclimated to the friends new Babylonian names.

Now read Daniel 3. Summarize the story that we see here.

What do we learn about the three friends' walk with God in this passage?

What do we learn about God from this passage?

More and more you will find yourself in situations that will resonate with how it might have felt to be Daniel and his three friends.

I have talked with several students at our church about what it's like to be a Christ-follower in today's school system, and they shared with me how difficult it is to not bow to popularity or conformity but to live daily for Christ. Here is what I've found to be true and see in the above stories:

1. *Our daily walk with God impacts our toughest moments.* What you do in your quiet time impacts what happens as you go to school. You never know when your moment to endure and persevere through temptation or trial will come, so prepare every day to refuse to bow to these pressures.

2. *Walking with others who walk with God will help you endure.* See what happened with Daniel and his friends? When we stand by ourselves, it is much more difficult to endure.

ENDURANCE

Have you ever run a race? A few years ago, I signed up to run a half-marathon with a few friends. This is an easier choice for some than it was for me. I had sustained a double foot surgery in years prior due to some mechanics of my feet that had gotten much worse as I played college soccer. To walk or run more than five miles would leave me in excruciating pain even after the surgeries. I have a metal pin in one foot, and while it does allow me to know when rainstorms are approaching, it, along with the scars, is a reminder that I have horrible feet.

When I was recovering from the surgeries, I remember praying that God would knit my bones back together just like He could do when He made me. I remember having to surrender control to Him and wondered if I'd ever be able to walk again without a limp.

The time came for me to run the half-marathon. I had been training with my friend Amy. Amy and I had been able to run all the way up to about 10 miles in our previous trainings. During the race Amy used a pace clock to tell me when to speed up and when to slow down. When I wanted to quit she would say things like, "I've run this course before. If you get to the top of the hill where that blue house is, it will be flat for about three miles." She would tell me when water stations were close by. She would smack my hand when I tried to eat something from the race stations that we had not trained with. She said, "You can't eat that! We don't know what that could do to your body. It's untested race food." I may or may not have wanted to trip her a couple of times during the race, but I could not have run that race without her.

At one point when I wanted to stop she told me stories of her dad who was a master marathon runner. She said, "you know what my dad tells me? He says you can do anything for 10 minutes. We only have one mile left and that's about 10 minutes." That's all I needed to keep going. And then as we approached the finish line, my friend even told me where the cameras were so that if I wanted to smile as I crossed the finish line, I could. Guess what? I didn't smile. I looked like I was glaring at my friend Amy as we ran through it together.

I endured that race because I had someone with me who shared the same goal. She was going the same way as me. She knew how to encourage me.

NOW WHAT?

We need accountability partners to run this race with us so we can endure. Paul mentions races in Scripture as a reminder of how we are to run this race called life.

Read 1 Corinthians 9:24.

"Don't you know that the runners in a stadium all race, but only one receives the prize? Run in such a way to win the prize."

How does the above verse translate to the Christian walk? What does this have to do with running with endurance?

Read 2 Timothy 4:7.

"I have fought the good fight, I have finished the race, I have kept the faith."

PAUL

Think about how Paul might have felt while he was in prison. What did he hold onto that allowed him to finish the race?

Paul wrote this in a letter while he was sitting in prison. But not just any prison. He had been dropped down a hole to sit in extremely cramped confines with winter approaching. He knew this was most likely the end of his time and death was approaching. And yet, at the end of his life he could celebrate that he had endured.

What was Paul's secret to finishing the race and keeping the faith in the midst of so many trials and temptations to give up?

Read Hebrews 12:1-2.

1 Therefore, since we also have such a large cloud of witnesses surrounding us, let us lay aside every weight and the sin that so easily ensnares us. Let us run with endurance the race that lies before us, **2** keeping our eyes on Jesus, the source and perfecter of our faith, who for the joy that lay before Him endured a cross and despised the shame and has sat down at the right hand of God's throne.

Endurance is impossible without the right focus. Your focus must not be on your future. Your focus must not be on who will take you to prom. Rather, your focus must be on Christ. If that relationship is the center of your life, then you will find the ability to endure daily.

On Your Own

CREATIVE PROCESS

Who is on your endurance team? Paul had friends that encouraged him to keep going. We saw the importance of the friendships Daniel had. So today, before we leave this session on endurance, pray about who will be on your endurance team.

Much like a pit crew for a race car driver, we need some specialized people to come alongside us and help us persevere in the race. Once you have determined your crew, figure out a way to ask them to be on your team. Tell them what your expectations are for that. For me, I have a group of girls and women that will meet with me at regularly scheduled times to pray for me and with me. I have others that have the right to ask me questions at any time to determine what's going on in my life.

Tell them that you value them and want them to help you commit to enduring this faith walk. I promise you, these relationships will be treasured for years to come.

CREATIVE ADVENTURE

Your creative adventure for today is this:

Use markers to write a verse on your feet that will remind you about the race you are running every day with your life.

Share a picture of your feet with that verse on social media using the hashtag: **#runtherace**.

PRAYER

Read and meditate on Hebrews 12:1-2. Pray that God would help you endure as you run the race, and that He would keep your eyes focused on Christ. Thank God for sacrificing His one and only Son for our sins. Consider what He endured on the cross and be willing and ready for how God wants to use you to make an impact in your school, home, or the world.

Biblical Womanhood

1 PETER 2:9

"But you are a chosen race, a royal priesthood, a holy nation, a people for His possession, so that you may proclaim the praises of the One who called you out of darkness into His marvelous light."

WELCOME

You've made it to the final session, girls! I'm so proud of you and thankful for your commitment to studying God's Word. During the last session we looked at the lives of Joseph, Daniel, and Paul, and how they showed perseverance in the midst of difficulty. This session, we'll wrap up the study as we look at what the Bible says about how we're to live as young women in the church.

Press Play

As you watch the Session 8 video, consider God's plans for you and how He might want to use you to impact your family, school, and community for Christ.

DISCUSS

As you reflect on the last session, in what area of your life do you need to have more endurance?

How is God working in your life or in the lives of others in your group?

What does "ordained" mean?

What does "royal priesthood" mean according to 1 Peter 2:9? How are you living a "set apart" life at school and at home?

If you've trusted in Christ as your Savior, this verse also says that God "called you out of darkness." How is that evidenced in your daily life?

Let's Talk

CULTURE

There is much to be said to girls and women these days about biblical womanhood. In fact, much IS said to us regarding our identity, significance, and purpose. Oftentimes the church is left fumbling to pass along the message of biblical womanhood in the midst of all the other messages in our lives.

We are shaped daily by culture, media, peers, personal experiences, and family. If you are not rooted in truth, it will cause you to misunderstand your identity, significance, and purpose as a girl and a woman. As a girls' minister, I want to do everything I can to help you develop a rock solid foundation built on Christ first and foremost. Why? Because when we are rooted in Him, then everything about us flows out of the truth of who Christ is and who Christ says we are.

In the fall of 2014, the hashtag *#pottymouthprincesses* was seen trending on social media. The hashtag was started by a radical feminist group that had utilized young girls to deliver their message to the masses. The reason it was so controversial was because the message used girls dressed as princesses discussing inequalities for women amongst vulgar cuss words and shocking statements. Their point was that people were more shocked by the obscene language used than they were about the message and statements.

I was recently asked what I thought about all of this commotion, as this feminist group considered the campaign a success for their cause. My response was that this was a strong reminder for us as parents, girls ministers, sisters, daughters, and the church that we have a responsibility to make sure that the voice of Christ is heard over the voices of our culture. We are called to submit to live out the movement Christ has ordained for us.

I know that in a church context, the word "ordained" may ruffle feathers, but let's look at that word for a moment. Ordain means: to make (someone) a priest or minister; confer holy orders (priestly robes) on.

We've looked at this verse already in the opening session. As we close out this study, let's take a look at it again.

> But you are a chosen race, a royal priesthood, a holy nation, a people for His possession, so that you may proclaim the praises of the One who called you out of darkness into His marvelous light. **–1 PETER 2:9**

Go ahead and draw a little crown over the words "royal priesthood" and then also over each "you" that you see in that passage.

This passage was given to both men and women, sons and daughters, and boys and girls that belong to Him. We often hear the word priest and may think it excludes girls or women. However, this is inclusive of both male and female. It isn't the first time we hear a message like this in Scripture. This is a very important passage for you and for me.

IDENTITY IN CHRIST

Let's not overlook the importance of this ordinance on your life as His precious daughter. We'll start by taking a brief overview of the whole story, starting out in the garden where it all began.

CONSEQUENCES OF THE FALL

1. *The first consequence was the separation of humanity from God.*

Draw a stick figure with a lightning bolt next to it, then write the word *God* to signify the separation from humanity from God.

2. *The earth began to rebel and revolt against humanity.*

Draw a world with a lightning bolt next to it, then draw your stick figure again on the other side of the lightning bolt to symbolize the separation from the world and humanity.

Number two here represents how humanity warred with the earth and started seeing weeds and destruction in ways they hadn't seen before.

3. *The third effect of sin was that we were separated from one another.*

Draw a stick figure with a lightning bolt next to it and then draw another stick figure on the other side of the lightning bolt to symbolize the separation between all of humanity.

Now let's read a little story about a tower.

Read Genesis 11:1-9.

As humanity had begun to populate, it is interesting to note that there was still one universal language. The tower of Babel is important because following this story in humanity, we would no longer live as a cohesive unit. Humanity tried to reach God on their own, and so they were separated. They became confused and had many different languages, no longer able to work together.

ABRAM

Next chapter. The very next story is about God coming to man. One man, in fact. A man named Abram, later to be named Abraham.

God calls Abram to be a person . . . to be His people.

Read Exodus 19:3-6.

From this passage, we learn that God has a mission, a purpose, an identity for the Israelites.

Now read Exodus 6:28–7:2.

Who was God's choice for sending Pharaoh messages from Him?

I'm going to make you like God to Pharaoh. It does not say I'm going to give you some tracts or I'm going to give you a song or a drama, but rather, I'm going to make you like God. Moses himself became the message to Pharaoh. God chose to show up to Pharaoh in the form of a human being.

Return to Exodus 19:3-6.

So we're at the base of Mt. Sinai and the Israelites have just been liberated. God is saying to them, "You were in Egypt—I rescued you, I redeemed you, and I brought you out. Now that you are redeemed, liberated, and rescued, I don't just want you roaming the earth without a purpose. I have rescued you because I have a plan for who I want you to be and what I want you to do."

You are to be a kingdom of Priests. Whoa, this sounds familiar, doesn't it?

WHAT IS A PRIEST?

A priest puts the divine on display. If you were to go into a temple and you wanted to know what the god they worship is all about you would look at their priests. I actually do this with students every summer when we visit a place in Vancouver called god road. It is a place where literally next door to each other on one road are several different world religions in their temples or places of worship. We go in and make appointments with the priests. That's how we find out about their religion or their god.

Same thing was true back in Old Testament times. You would take note as to how the priest acted, how the priest lived, how the priest dressed. If you wanted to find out how their god worked in the world, you would find out from that god's priests.

So the Israelites were liberated from slavery and oppression not just to be a part of the liberated club, but to display God to the world. This is the first time in world history that God has appeared to a group of people. This was unheard of. God had appeared to individual persons but not to a group of people.

Two invitations are being given to the people at Mt. Sinai:

In the body of the letter, create an invitation that shows God's people are invited to do two things: They are invited to meet with God and they are invited to be His message to the world.

Flip over to Joshua 3 where God's people go to the promised land. Israel rejected this invitation to His message to the world. Instead, they wanted to be like the other kingdoms around them. As a result, they missed out on displaying God to the rest of the world.

Then read Philippians 2:1-11 and Hebrews 4:15.

So Jesus embraced the mission that the Israelites rejected. Jesus took on human form and became our high priest. He puts God on display to the world and brings man to God.

That was a quick overview, but it's important to your mission that is given to the church in 1 Peter. See, this was given after the message of good news that the tomb was empty and Jesus had risen.

So, what now? The world sees an empty tomb and they want to know where God is. This is the thing that ties us in with being a royal priesthood. We are invited to represent Christ to a lost and dying world. We are to be the hands and feet of Christ! We are to bear the message with our lives that He has heard our cry and has redeemed us!

The message is contained in our lives and is brought forth with the Holy Spirit at work within us. This is why personal holiness is such a precious gift and pursuit.

 KEEP IT 100 **When we realize that we are the body of Christ, shouldn't that impact the way we live with that body? List some specific ways that should change how we live in community with other believers.**

HOLY ORDERS

You are a part of that royal priesthood, so you have to acknowledge that as Christ followers we are given holy orders. Let that sink in for a moment.

So one of the first messages you need to know is that if Christ reigns in your heart, then you are a royal priesthood. This impacts our purpose at the very core of who we are. Now if I know you like I know me, you are probably really liking the royal priesthood title.

It is important that you understand that while you are ordained, you are not entitled. We live in a world shouting at us as girls and women to embrace our inner princess and use our reign to do anything—even display foul-mouthed vulgarity to get our way.

> Settle down there, Little Miss Tiara. That's not the kind of royal life we're talking about here.

PURITY

Girls, God has uniquely conferred holy orders (priestly garments) on you that are specific to women, but it does not leave you as spoiled princesses in His Kingdom. God has specific work for us to do as girls and as women.

Scripture is clear in how women are supposed to pass these truths along when it says "train the younger women to... " (Titus 2:4, ESV). The word "train" in this passage is the Greek word *sóphronizó,* which means to "encourage" or "urge."[1]

That word *encourage* is one we use a lot, but when you look at a definition, it truly gives some insight into what it looks like to teach biblical womanhood.

> en·cour·age·ment (noun)
> To give courage to; to inspire with courage, spirit, or hope; to raise, or to increase the confidence of; to animate; to enhearten; to incite; to help forward." [2]

I love that phrase, "to help forward." This means that older women and spiritually mature girls are to encourage girls younger than them in their pursuit of Christ.

Biblical womanhood doesn't start with a fashion show or handing out a tiara labeled with a sticker that says "God's little princess." Biblical Womanhood starts with *you* knowing that *you* were created in His image and your identity is being transformed by the work of Christ in and through you. That's the message that is central to your work of encouraging and urging your sisters in Christ as you walk alongside the girls God has placed in your life.

TITUS 2 INSTRUCTIONS

So then, what does it look like to walk alongside other girls and young women in the specifics of biblical womanhood? When you drill down deeper into Titus 2 and what Paul lists for women to train other women in, you see six distinct instructions that were given to these women.

Now there are many conversations going on in the church regarding hot topics on biblical womanhood that Paul touches on ranging from submission, to stay at home moms, and working moms, etc. My aim is not for us to get hung up on these conversations, but to remember that there is womanhood rooted in Christ and there is womanhood not rooted in Christ. These areas of instruction served as guardrails to ensure women were not getting off track in their pursuits.

The six areas of instruction that Paul addressed deal with three primary areas: the home, relationships with family, and the overflow of our own hearts.

Check them out!

1. to love their husbands and children
2. to be self-controlled
3. to be pure
4. to be working at home
5. to be kind
6. to be submissive to their own husbands

When you recognize that your identity, significance, and purpose is rooted in Christ and not in those three areas, then you can see how influential a girl can be when she lives out her holy orders in these distinct ways. But if a girl begins living *for* those specific spheres of influence or roles without recognizing her holy orders, then you see unbiblical womanhood taking shape. These are channels to live out her holy orders . . . the channels are not themselves to be her God. God has uniquely gifted and called women to be a part of His kingdom work and shine Christ through these channels and roles.

The alternative to a womanhood centered on Christ is a womanhood not centered on Christ. One area this crops up in is feminism. Feminism is in a battle to gain territory and rights for women. Biblical womanhood rooted in Christ's love is a revolution to set all people free from death and sin to live in the freedom that only Christ can bring. I believe that biblical womanhood rooted in Christ's love is radical in that it brings a dignity and life to women that feminism could never provide. So all the messages that are dangled in front of women and girls to get them to ignore their holy orders and identity can be wrapped up in this pursuit of "what a girl wants."

NOW WHAT?

Several years ago there was a popular song by Christina Aguilera titled "What a Girl Wants."

So what does a girl want these days in our culture? Selfie likes? A diamond ring? A baby? The beauty of her youth?

Take a moment to discuss this with the girls in your group. Use emojis to draw out the answers below.

These wants and likes may seem different from those of the very first girl in the Bible, but it still came down to a battle of the wants with Eve. She discovered what was at stake when she ignored God's will, pursued her own will, and snatched fruit from the forbidden tree. Even today these pursuits ultimately leave us empty and enslaved.

This can be seen when a woman flips her focus from Christ to finding her identity in the three spheres mentioned earlier.

Biblical womanhood that is rooted in Christ's love recognizes that we are a royal priesthood with a mission to praise the One who brought us out of darkness, gave us life, and set us free.

So as we live out these holy orders with the gifting and uniqueness of women, may our praises ring out to others who are walking in darkness. And may they turn to Christ because they see evidence of His love at work in our lives channeled through the specific roles He has given us as we love others through the sphere of influence He has called us to.

On Your Own

CREATIVE PROCESS

Take the below outline of a paper doll and make her look like you. Label her a "royal priesthood."

Consider what that means for your life in the three primary circles of influence that God gives us as girls and women:

home   relationships   the overflow of our own hearts

CREATIVE ADVENTURE

Cut out your paper doll and like you would do with a "Flat Stanley," take her on a documented journey wherever you go this week. How does it change your ordinary day to know you have an extraordinary God who has ordained you with His message to the world? How will you share that? How will that impact your everyday ordinary moments? How will that impact your relationships? Use the hashtag: *#iamaroyalpriesthood*

PRAYER

Ask God to make you more like Him, but also to teach you about biblical womanhood. Consider how Titus 2 instructs older women to mentor younger women. Think about who is already a mentor to you, as well as someone you could mentor.

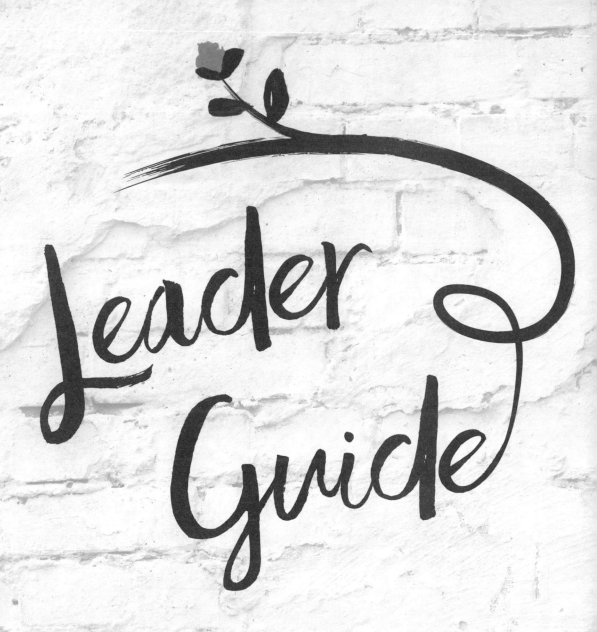

Leader Guide

THANK YOU!

First of all, thank you for your commitment to lead girls through this study! We are praying for you and want you to know you are not alone in this. Thank you for giving of your time and of your resources to serve guys and to point them to Christ. Our hope and prayer is that they will understand God's love for them in Christ and that they will daily offer their bodies as living sacrifices to Him.

HOW TO LEAD A GIRLS' BIBLE STUDY

If this is your first time or your 50th time to lead a girls' BIble study, we want to help you guide the girls in your group through God's Word. The videos are an important component, so try to designate at least 10 minutes for viewing the videos from Amy-Jo at the beginning of each session.

We've included the *Main Point/Objective* of each session at the top of each page in following Leader Guide, as well as some *Leader Prep* helps. Do not feel like you have to cover all of the options and questions included in the Leader Guide, but rather use it as a guide and a starting point for your group discussion.

Get Started will give you some tips for opening the session. This is also a good time to recap the previous session and introduce what will be covered in the current session as well. Then *Press Play* and watch the video for the session you are in, and that should be followed up with discussion.

There are a few different ways you can approach the *On Your Own* section. Most of you will probably be short on time, so it will be best for girls to take their books home to complete this section during the week. If you do conclude the session early though, go ahead and give girls the opportunity to complete this at the end of the session.

TRUE LOVE WAITS HISTORY AND INFO

About twenty years ago a small group of students in the Nashville area committed themselves to Christ in the pursuit of purity. Little did they know that shortly thereafter there were going to be thousands of additional students join them in what came to be known as the movement of *True Love Waits*.

Over the years *True Love Waits* has witnessed hundreds of thousands of young people commit their sexual purity to God, while at the same time offering the promise of hope and restoration in Christ for all who have sinned sexually. It has been a tremendous movement, orchestrated by God, to further spread the biblical message of sex and purity to a younger generation.

There is a Commitment Card in the back of this study that you can use with your group. Remind girls that this is a serious commitment to personal holiness. Don't pressure your students to make this commitment, but use this as a tool to generate conversation and lead your students to embrace the power of accountability in their pursuit of Christ through Christian community.

To purchase additional commitment cards, see *lifeway.com/truelovewaits*.

Session 1: The Best Possible You

MAIN POINT/OBJECTIVE

Girls will be challenged to realize that the only way they can be the best possible version of themselves is by following God and His plans for their lives. Our culture tells us we are to look perfect on social media, but God's Word reminds us that we are to be holy as He is holy (1 Pet. 1:15-16). Pursuing holiness is not easy, but following Christ is worth it.

LEADER PREP

- Prior to your meeting, read through Session 1, highlighting and taking notes on what you want to cover with the girls in your group during this session. During this study, girls will be challenged to find their worth and identity in Christ, which will lead them to live lives of purity.

- Prepare a class contact list to pass around for girls to fill in (if they choose to do so). Explain that this will allow you to send updates and keep in touch with them during the week. Consider including these columns for them to fill out (name, phone number/email, social media platform you like best, favorite candy).

- One other idea is to provide a box or jar for the girls to share their prayer requests with you and the group. There are several ways to do this, but the first step is to provide a container to collect prayer requests in each week. Shuffle the requests, then instruct each girl to draw one prayer request from the container as they leave each week.

GET STARTED

Introduce yourself and briefly get to know the girls in your group. If you know in advance that there are a lot of girls in your group who do not know each other, you might want to plan an Icebreaker activity to allow them to get to know each other better. Remind girls of the schedule and that this is an 8-week commitment. Encourage them to take it seriously and be prayerful about what God might want to teach them.

PRESS PLAY

Set up and make sure the video system is working in advance so that it is ready for you to simply press play. Watch the Session 1 video (included in the DVD Kit). Allow time for discussion after. There are discussion questions on page 9 specifically designed to go along with Session 1's video.

LET'S TALK

This time of discussion will build on the video guide discussion on page 9. As you dive further into the topics and themes that were introduced in this session's video, consider working in some of the following discussion questions.

- In our culture, who do you tend to look up to? Who's Insta feed are you looking at the most?
- How is your identity shaped by the culture? By God? What areas of your life do you need to surrender to the Lord's control?
- When we find our worth and identity in Christ, we will honor Him with our bodies. Do your classmates and friends identify you as a Christ follower by how you live your life? If not, examine your heart and ask God to help you to point others to Him.

ON YOUR OWN

This section is designed for girls to complete at the end of your group discussion if time allows. If you are pressed for time, then encourage girls to complete this section during the week as they reflect on what they have studied so far. Suggest that they find somewhere quiet and relaxing where they can spend time with God thinking about and processing what it means to live a life of holiness.

FOLLOW-UP

Refer back to the contact list you passed around and use it to keep in touch with the girls in your group this week. Set up a group message or email to remind them of the Scripture from the session, or just send girls individual encouragement based on what you know they are going through.

NOTES

Session 2: Our Identity in Christ

MAIN POINT/OBJECTIVE

This session will help girls understand their identity in Christ. It will address who or what culture tells them they need to be versus who God says they are.

LEADER PREP

- Prior to your meeting, read back over Session 1 and think about any questions girls asked or things they discussed that you want to cover more thoroughly this session. Then read through Session 2, highlighting and taking notes on what you want to cover with the girls in your group during your time together.

- In this session, Amy-Jo talks about identity, so if it fits well for your group, consider playing Matthew West's song "Hello, My Name Is" (*Into the Light*, 2012) that points to how we are children of the one, true King. This might be a good song to have ready to play in the background as girls are arriving.

GET STARTED

Remind girls that they are no longer defined by lies, regrets, or what this world has to say, but that we have Christ's autograph all over us. Our identity is in Him if we have submitted our lives to Jesus Christ.

PRESS PLAY

Watch the Session 2 video (included in the DVD Kit). Allow time for discussion after. There are discussion questions on page 19 specifically designed to go along with Session 2's video.

LET'S TALK

This time of discussion will build on the video guide discussion on page 19. As you dig deeper into the topics and themes that were introduced in this session's video, consider working in some of the following discussion questions.

- Discuss the *Real Beauty* campaign more in-depth with the girls in the group. If girls are not familiar with it, you might search for a clip to show from the campaign for further explanation. Then, talk about the mixed messages our world sends and how these messages are often not in line with what God's Word tells us about our identity and where forgiveness is found. What does the world tell us we should place our identity in as girls? What messages do magazines and social media send about beauty and our identity?

- Are you continually striving for good works, or are you finding your worth and identity in Christ? Explain.
- How is your life set apart and different from the world? In this session, you read about how the word *Christian* means "little Christ." What does this mean for you? How do you need to model your life to be more like Christ?

FOLLOW-UP

Be mindful of the girls in your group and their busy schedules and lives. This does not mean that you need to avoid contacting them, but don't go overboard with sending texts. Be sure they have your contact info and know that you are available any time they want to talk.

This week, try to get to know each girl a little bit better. Ask them about their interests, maybe what their favorite movie is or what they like to do for fun. Pray that this might lead you to a discussion of their spiritual gifts and where they might be able to serve in the church if they already know Christ as their Lord and Savior.

Pray for the girls in your group all throughout the week, specifically asking God to prepare their hearts for the next session on forgiveness and redemption. Also confess any sin in your own heart and life, and ask God to give you wisdom and discernment as you talk with girls about heavy matters and other things they may want to discuss with you. Seek to give them a biblical response. If you are unsure about a question they have, explain that you will get back to them with an answer.

ON YOUR OWN

This section is designed for girls to complete at the end of your meeting time if time allows. If you are pressed for time, then encourage girls to complete this section during the week as they reflect on what they have studied so far.

NOTES

Session 3: Forgiveness and Redemption

MAIN POINT/OBJECTIVE

This session focuses on restoration, and it begins by introducing how there is a fascination with transformation in our culture. As believers, our identity in Christ reveals an even more incredible transformation. Before we come to knowo Christ we are lost and in sin, but after we come to know Christ as Lord and Savior, we have forgiveness and we are redeemed by His blood.

LEADER PREP

- Before your meeting, read back over Session 2 and think about any questions girls asked or things they discussed that you want to cover more thoroughly this session. Then read through Session 3, highlighting and taking notes on what you want to cover with the girls in your group.

- Pray for the girls in your group by name using the contact list from Session 1. Be prepared to stay after this session to talk with girls who might want to know more about how they can become a Christ follower if they do not already know Him as Lord and Savior.

GET STARTED

Remind girls that they can bring a journal or notebook for any extra notes they may want to take, but that this is optional. It might also be a good idea to provide some blank paper and pencils or pens for girls who do not have a journal to take notes in.

As you begin, keep in mind that some girls may have difficult pasts and still struggle with regrets. Be mindful of this as you talk about forgiveness and redemption. Guide discussion back to Scripture if girls get off topic. Be encouraging and remind girls of how God sent His only Son to forgive our sins and provide redemption.

PRESS PLAY

Watch the Session 3 video (included in the DVD Kit). Allow time for discussion after. There are discussion questions on page 29 specifically designed to go along with the Session 3 video from Amy-Jo.

LET'S TALK

This time of discussion will build on the video guide discussion on page 29. As you dive further into the topics and themes that were introduced in this session's video, consider working in some of the following discussion questions.

- Discuss the idea of restoration and how we enjoy seeing and hearing about transformation that takes place. Why do we love watching shows like *Fixer Upper* and hearing stories of transformation?

- Share your testimony (your life before and after Christ) with the group. Share how God has transformed your life and how He continues to shape and mold you into His image. Allow girls to ask questions. If time allows, give several volunteers the opportunity to share how Christ has changed their lives.

- How does Christ's forgiveness and redemption cover all of our sins? Give girls some time to pray on their own, thanking God for sending Jesus. Also guide them to spend some time praying. Encourage them to make confession a part of their daily lives.

FOLLOW-UP

Contact any girls in your group during the week who wanted to know more about a personal relationship with Jesus. Pray for them specifically this week. Then, pray and ask God to help all of the girls in your group to know true forgiveness and redemption in Christ.

ON YOUR OWN

This section is designed for girls to complete at the end of your meeting time if time allows. If you are pressed for time, then encourage girls to complete this section during the week as they reflect on what they have studied so far.

NOTES

Session 4: What does love look like?

MAIN POINT/OBJECTIVE

God is the author and perfecter of love. God is love, so we must look to Him and not to the world for our definition of what love is. Encourage girls to dig deep into God's Word and to examine their hearts for any idols—anyone or anything that they love and put before God in their life.

LEADER PREP

- Prior to your meeting, read back over Session 3 and think about any questions girls asked or things they discussed that you want to cover more thoroughly this session. Then read through Session 4, highlighting and taking notes on what you want to cover with the girls in your group during this session.

- This might be a sensitive subject for girls who may not feel loved. If you like to bake, you might consider bringing a sweet treat for your group this week. Or if you are artsy, you might make some sort of craft with this week's verse on it for each girl. Make this a special time for the girls in your group—help them to know you love and care about them.

GET STARTED

Begin this session by reminding girls of Christ's love for them and the worth He sees in each of them. Be mindful that some girls may be in serious relationships while some girls in your group may have never dated. Try not to make relationships the focus of discussion, but rather personal holiness and a heart that follows after God.

Share challenges you faced as a teen or as a young adult and by doing so, encourage and challenge the girls in your group to glorify God with their bodies.

PRESS PLAY

Be mindful that Amy-Jo discusses sex, so set the tone of this session accordingly. If you have some girls in your group who are not as mature, encourage the group as a whole to take this video seriously.

Watch the Session 4 video (included in the DVD Kit). Allow time for discussion after. There are discussion questions on page 39 specifically designed to go along with Session 4's video.

LET'S TALK

This time of discussion will build on the video guide discussion on page 39. As you dig deepr into the topics and themes that were introduced in this session's video, consider working in some of the following discussion questions.

- How do most of your classmates and friends view love?
- What does 1 John 4:16 say about love? What does this mean for us as believers? How are we supposed to love others?
- How does this affect our purity and our commitment to holiness? Explain.

FOLLOW-UP

Sometime during the week, send out a message or text to girls reminding and challenging them to holiness. Remind the girls in your group that our actions stem from the heart, so we need to daily examine our hearts and motives, asking God for forgiveness for sin in our lives.

Consider sending out a reminder or posting 1 John 4:16 on your own social media this week. Encourage the girls in your group to commit this verse to memory this week.

ON YOUR OWN

This section is designed for girls to complete at the end of your meeting if time allows. If you are pressed for time, encourage girls to complete this section during the week as they reflect on what they have studied so far.

NOTES

Session 5: What is humility?

MAIN POINT/OBJECTIVE

When we look at lordship, we must determine who is on the throne of our lives. As believers, we will ultimately lay our crowns at Jesus' feet, so we must seek to serve His kingdom and His purposes. We must exchange our pride for humility and clothe ourselves with humility each and every day.

LEADER PREP

- Before your meeting, read back over Session 4 and think about any questions girls asked or things they discussed that you want to cover more thoroughly this session. Then read through Session 5, highlighting and taking notes on what you want to work through with the girls in your group during this session.

- If you are not familiar with the term "humblebrag," you might want to search the hashtag *#humblebrag* on social media to get a general idea of what this means and what sort of posts would be considered humblebrags. Amy-Jo explains it in the Session 5 video as well.

GET STARTED

Our culture in general tends to be very focused on ourselves, so start by discuss why that is and emphasize how Jesus models true humility for us in Scripture. Read Isaiah 66:1-2 aloud or ask a girl to read it for everyone to hear.

PRESS PLAY

Watch the Session 5 video (included in the DVD Kit). Amy-Jo shares about how we've become obsessed with being the star of our own story, but that's not what life is really all about. Allow time for discussion. There are discussion questions on page 49 specifically designed to go along with Session 5's video.

LET'S TALK

This time of discussion will build on the video guide questions included on page 49. As you dive further into the topics and themes that were introduced in this session's video, consider working in some of the following discussion questions.

- Pride is the opposite of humility. How do we see an attitude of pride in our culture? On TV? On social media? In the news?

- Why is it so easy for us to become focused on our own plans and agenda, or our wants and needs, rather than focusing on our identity in Christ?
- Read Colossians 3:12 and discuss what this verse means. Challenge girls to clothe themselves with humility each and every day.

FOLLOW-UP

During the week, pray for the girls in your group by name. You are more than half-way through leading this study, so keep pressing on!

As women, we tend to be chatty and sometimes we struggle with the sin of gossip. We speak harshly about the failures and weaknesses of others so that we might look better by comparison. Think about how you tend to talk about yourself and how you talk about others. Do you promote yourself, or are you generally focused on the needs and interests of others? Seek to apply the truths of Scripture to your life and seek accountability with another adult if you do not already have someone to hold you accountable and to encourage you in your walk with the Lord.

Sometime this week, send a message out to the girls in your group reminding them of Colossians 3:12 and how we are to clothe ourselves in humility. Pray for the girls in your group as they face a world that tells them that life is all about their needs and wants. Ask God to help them find their identity in Him and not in the mixed messages of this world.

ON YOUR OWN

This section is designed for girls to complete at the end of your meeting time if time allows. If you are pressed for time, then encourage girls to complete this section during the week as they reflect on what they have studied so far.

NOTES

Session 6: Surrender to Self-Sacrifice

MAIN POINT/OBJECTIVE

Christ has modeled self-sacrifice for us, so sacrifice should be evidenced in our lives. Romans 12:1 challenges us to present ourselves to God as living sacrifices. This is a daily surrender of our plans and dreams to His plans and His will for our lives. In this session, girls will also be challenged to pursue purity as they live for Christ. This will sometimes require making sacrifices, but God's purposes and plans are bigger and better than all of our own plans.

LEADER PREP

Before your meeting, read back over Session 5. If time allows, watch the Session 6 video in advance and read through the Session 6 content, highlighting and taking notes on what you want to cover with the girls in your group during this session.

GET STARTED

Start by sharing a story of self-sacrifice. Maybe a time when you gave of your time or resources in order to help someone who had a need. Recap last session's focus on humility and explain that when we humble ourselves and are seek God first, then we will naturally put others' needs before our own.

PRESS PLAY

Watch the Session 6 video (included in the DVD Kit). Allow time for discussion after. There are discussion questions on page 59 specifically designed to go along with Session 6's video.

LET'S TALK

This time of discussion will build on the video guide discussion on page 59. As you dig deeper into the topics and themes that were introduced in this session's video, consider working in some of the following discussion questions.

- In sports we see how athletes dedicate themselves to training and often make many sacrifices as they travel and are away from their families, all so they can compete. Why do you think they sacrifice so much to compete in a certain sport?
- Amy-Jo talks about the term *Christian* and how it means "little Christ." Read Acts 11:26 as a group. Then ask the girls if those closest to them (family and friends) would describe them as a "little Christ"? Why or why not?

- How and why does Christ call us to a life of holiness? Think about how you are seeking purity and holiness in your daily life. Share some of the challenges you face as you seek to be pure in a culture that often does what's right in its own eyes rather than what's right according to God's Word.

FOLLOW-UP

Encourage girls to surrender their lives fully to Jesus if they have not already. The girls in your group may have school activities or college applications vying for their time. Remind them of the importance of their relationship with Christ, and challenge them to make Him the first priority in their lives.

Consider the pressures the girls in your life might face to live a life of purity in their schools, on sports teams, and even in their churches. It will not always be easy, but remind them that God loves them and that living for Him is worth it.

Be available outside of the session meeting time to talk with the girls in your group. Be mindful that their lives and the pressures they face may be different than what you experienced as a teen. Pray that God will give you wisdom as you seek to point girls to Christ. Ask for His strength to make whatever sacrifices He might be calling you to make this week.

ON YOUR OWN

This section is designed for girls to complete at the end of your meeting time if time allows. If you are pressed for time, encourage girls to complete this section during the week as they reflect on what they have studied so far.

NOTES

Session 7: Running the Race

MAIN POINT/OBJECTIVE

Our daily walk with God impacts our daily endurance. As believers, we are to find our strength and endurance in Christ. Walking with others who walk with God gives us focus and strength through the trials of life. Christian friends encourage us and help point us back to Christ when we are struggling. Girls will be challenged to find accountability and encouragement from others who are walking with Christ.

LEADER PREP

- Before your meeting, read back over Session 6 and think about anything your group discussed that you want to review this session. Then read through Session 7, highlighting and taking notes on what you want to cover with the girls in your group during this session.

GET STARTED

Recap last session's theme of self-sacrifice. Challenge girls to live sacrificially and to put others before themselves. Give some practical examples of how they can do this in their day-to-day lives. A couple examples would be making their brother or sister's bed for them, or helping a parent wash the dishes. Explain that we must examine our motives and serve because of our love for God, not because we think we are good or want to earn God's love. We know that God loves us unconditionally and He gave everything on the cross, so we are to give our lives to worship Him.

Then transition into what we'll be discussing today by sharing an example of a time in your life when you needed to endure and persevere in your faith. Tell girls if you think you handled this trial with endurance, or if you became weak and would have handled this situation differently in retrospect.

PRESS PLAY

Watch the Session 7 video (included in the DVD Kit). Allow time for discussion after. There are discussion questions on page 69 specifically designed to go along with Session 7's video.

LET'S TALK

This time of discussion will build on the video guide discussion on page 69. As you dive further into the topics and themes that were introduced in this session's video, consider working in some of the following discussion questions.

- Think about and discuss clothes and products that do not last and are even made to fall apart, as Amy-Jo mentions in this session's video. Why do you find more value in a product that lasts? Explain.

- Who are you surrounding yourself with? What does your team look like? Are they helping you to stay focused on Christ as Hebrews 12:2 challenges us to do?

- How can you endure day-by-day as you seek to live a life of holiness and purity? Who is your ultimate source of encouragement and hope? Pray that you will turn to God's Word for the answers you need when you are experiencing trials.

FOLLOW-UP

Encourage girls to finish strong this week and next as you all finish out this study. Pray for strength and endurance for the girls, as well as for yourself.

If there are girls in your group who are athletes or runners, next session you might ask them to share how they are able to endure and persevere as they race and train.

Share opportunities for service with the girls in your group. This could range from helping in the nursery at your church, to helping serve at a missions banquet, or helping a widow at the church with some errands around town. These service activities can be done as a group, or on their own. Whatever works best for the girls in the group.

ON YOUR OWN

This section is designed for girls to complete at the end of your meeting time if time allows. If you are pressed for time, then encourage girls to complete this section during the week as they reflect on what they have studied so far.

NOTES

Session 8: Biblical Womanhood

MAIN POINT/OBJECTIVE

In this final session, we'll look at God's plan and how He has uniquely designed us as girls and women. First Peter 2:9 tells us we are "a royal priesthood," which means He has ordained or set us apart with a specific purpose.

LEADER PREP

- Before you meet for this final session, read back over Session 7 and briefly review what your group discussed last week. Then read through Session 8, highlighting and taking notes on what you want to cover with the girls in your group during this session.

GET STARTED

If time allows, recap what you've studied since the very start of this Bible study. In Session 1 and 2 we talked about the best possible you and that no matter how hard we try, we can only be the best version of ourselves when we find our identity in Christ. In Session 3 we talked about how we are forgiven and redeemed by the blood of Christ. He loved us so much that He sent His one and only Son, Jesus. In Session 4, we learned that God is love and yet our world's definition of love fails to reflect His character. Session 5 and 6 covered humility and self-sacrifice and how God calls us to trade pride for humility and offer our bodies as living sacrifices. Last session we learned studied endurance and how we must keep our eyes on Christ as we run the race.

PRESS PLAY

Watch the Session 8 video (included in the DVD Kit). Allow time for discussion after. There are discussion questions on page 79 specifically designed to go along with Session 8's video.

LET'S TALK

This time of discussion will build on the video guide discussion on page 79. As you dig deeper into the topics and themes that were introduced in this session's video, consider working in some of the following discussion questions.

- How does our culture view women? What is our world telling us a woman's role is?
- For further study, read Proverbs 31:10-31 and list what it says a biblical woman's character looks like.
- Why is it important for us to seek purity as young women? God designed marriage as a gift between a man and a woman. Challenge those who desire to marry one day to take some time to pray for their potential future spouse. Pray that even now he will be seeking after God and drawing closer to Him.

FOLLOW-UP

As you close out the final session of this study, let the girls in your group know you are there for them if they would like to talk more. Provide them with your contact information if they do not already have it.

Continue to pray for all of the girls in your group. Ask God to guide and direct their paths, and to help them make wise decisions in their lives and in their relationships. Pray that they would long for and seek after holiness and clothe themselves with humility and love each and every day of their lives.

ON YOUR OWN

This section is designed for girls to complete at the end of your meeting time if time allows. If you are pressed for time, then encourage girls to complete this section during the week as they reflect on what they have studied so far.

NOTES

SOURCES

SESSION 1

1. filter, *Merriam-Webster,* 2016. Available online at http://www.merriam-webster.com/dictionary/filter.

2. filter, *Online Etymology Dictionary,* 2016. Available online at http://www.etymonline.com/index.php?term=filter&allowed_in_frame=0.

3. Keep it 100, *definithing,* 2016. Available online at http://definithing.com/keep-it-100/.

SESSION 2

1. Our Research, *Unilever United States,* 2016. Available online at http://www.dove.com/us/en/stories/about-dove/our-research.html.

2. "Lexicon: Strong's H1254 - bara," *Blue Letter Bible,* accessed November 16, 2016, https://www.blueletterbible.org/lang/lexicon/lexicon.cfm?strongs=H1254.

3. "Lexicon: Strong's H3335 - yatsar," *Blue Letter Bible,* accessed November 16, 2016, https://www.blueletterbible.org/lang/lexicon/lexicon.cfm?strongs=H3335

4. The Image of God, *Ligonier Ministries,* 2016. Available online at http//www.lignoier.org/learn/devotionals/image-god/.

SESSION 3

1. Jon Ronson. "How One Stupid Tweet Blew Up Justine Sacco's Life." The New York Times. February 12, 2015, accessed November 14, 2016, http://www.nytimes.com/2015/02/15/magazine/how-one-stupid-tweet-ruined-justine-saccos-life.html.

2. Mike Glenn. *The Gospel of Yes: We Have Missed the Most Important Thing About God,* accessed November 16, 2016, https://books.google.com/books?isbn=0307730484.

3. "Strong's Concordance 2675 - kataritzo," Bible Hub, accessed November 16, 2016, http://biblehub.com/greek/2675.htm.

SESSION 5

1. humility, *Oxford University Press: Oxford Living Dictionaries,* 2016. Available online at https://en.oxforddictionaries.com/definition/humility.

2. BLOGHER, "The Definition of Humility," 2016. Available online at http://www.blogher.com/definition-humility.

3. humblebrag, *Macmillan Dictionary,* 2016. Available online at http://www.macmillandictionary.com/us/dictionary/american/humblebrag#humblebrag__1.

SESSION 6

1. @olympics. "Fair Play Awards Recognise True Olympic Champions in Sportsmanship." International Olympic Committee. August 20, 2016, accessed November 12, 2016, https://www.olympic.org/news/fair-play-awards-recognise-true-olympic-champions-in-sportsmanship.

2. @NBCOlympics. "Knee Injury Keeps Inspirational U.S. Runner Abbey D'Agostino from 5,000m Final." NBC Olympics. August 17, 2016, accessed November 14, 2016, http://www.nbcolympics.com/news/knee-injury-keeps-inspirational-us-runner-5000m-final.

3. Elisabeth Elliot. *Passion and Purity: Learning to Bring Your Love Life Under Christ's Control,* 90.

SESSION 8

1. "Strong's 4993 - sóphronizó," Bible Hub, accessed November 16, 2016, http://biblehub.com/greek/4994.htm.

2. encouragement, *Wordnik,* 2016. Available online at https://www.wordnik.com/words/encourage.

TRUE LOVE WAITS COMMITMENT

By the time you have reached this section, you have hopefully gone through all eight sessions of *Authentic Love*. It is our hope and prayer that by this point, the words on this commitment card are an accurate reflection of where your heart is right now in regard to your commitment to Christ in your pursuit of purity.

truelovewaits.
COMMITMENT

In light of who God is, what Christ has done for me, and who I am in Him, from this day forward I commit myself to Him in the lifelong pursuit of personal holiness. By His grace, I will continually present myself to Him as a living sacrifice, holy and pleasing to God.

Signature _____

Date _____

NOTES

NOTES

NOTES

NOTES

GIRLS MINISTRY RESOURCES

All Things New
By Kelly Minter

Over 8 sessions, Kelly Minter will lead girls through the Letter of 2 Corinthians to discover how Paul's encouragement to the believers in Corinth challenges the church and young women today. This Bible study also includes leader helps and 7 weeks of personal study to be completed between group sessions. As new creations in Christ, we are to spread the message of Jesus' grace, comfort, and generosity with the world. In the way we live, we must boldly declare that He makes all things new.

Student Book 005787455 $12.99

Worthy Vessel
By Amy Byrd

This six-session resource will lead girls through an in-depth study of 2 Timothy. They will examine biblical context and a multitude of spiritual truths in this letter from the apostle Paul to Timothy. As they explore the relationship between Paul and his young disciple, girls will be challenged to live as worthy vessels of the gospel of Jesus Christ, encouraging others to walk in faith as they deliver the message God has entrusted to them.

Student Book 006104413 $11.99
Downloadable Student eBook 005789762 $11.99
Leader Kit 006104400 $59.99
Digital Leader Kit 005792206 $59.99

Looking for Lovely
By Annie F. Downs

This seven-session study for middle-and high-school girls will challenge them to look for the lovely in the midst of trials. It is also designed to help girls persevere through those trials and grow in godly character and hope. Girls will study examples throughout the Bible of people who sought out the lovely in the midst of their everyday lives.

Student Book 005781390 $11.99
Downloadable Student eBook 006104392 $11.99
Digital Video Bundle 005788239 $24.99

More Than Pretty
By Ocielia Gibson

More Than Pretty is a six-session Bible study for teen girls that explores the definition of true beauty. Using our five natural senses, this resource will serve as a tool to guide girls in exploring how to spiritually and practically develop multifaceted beauty that ultimately honors God. This resource will also help girls better understand their identity in Christ, and the meaning of true beauty.

Student Book 006104384 $10.99
Downloadable Student eBook 005786808 $10.99
Leader Kit 006104383 $59.99

TO LEARN MORE OR PURCHASE, VISIT LIFEWAY.COM OR VISIT YOUR LOCAL LIFEWAY CHRISTIAN STORE.